Playful Pop-Up Cards

Hajimete no Pop-up Cards (Pop-up Cards for the First Time) (Lady Boutique Series no. 3130)
Originally published in Japanese language by Boutique-Sha, Inc.

First published in the United States of America by World Book Media, LLC
For information, address World Book Media LLC
134 Federal Street, Salem, MA 01970 USA
Email: info@worldbookmedia.com

WBM worldbookmedia

Japanese Edition
Author: Takami Suzuki
Editor: Tamami Miyazaki
Photographer: Ritsuko Fujita
Book Designer: Haniyo Sakai (t-head design)
Illustrations: Mai Shirai

English Edition
Translation: Kyoko Matthews
English Editors: Lindsay Fair and Genia Patestides
Production: Christy Bao

ISBN 978-0-9853747-0-9

First English edition August 2012

Printed in China.
10 9 8 7 6 5 4 3 2 1

Playful Cards

s for All Occasions

Takami Suzuki

Contents

Introduction

In this book you will find 25 beautiful pop-up cards designs that are fun to make and a delight to give away. At first glance, the designs in this book might look difficult, but they really aren't! With carefully sequenced step-by-step photos, clear instructions, and full-size project templates, you'll be amazed by how easy these cards are to construct. Also, no special tools or supplies are needed.

The colorful, whimsical cards in this collection feature versatile motifs suitable for a host of occasions or sentiments. Use these fun 3D card designs for birthdays, bat mitzvahs, graduations and Christmas greetings. Flowers, hearts, stars, sweets and holiday specific motifs are included for making handcrafted pop-up card for countless original greetings and messages.

Once you get accustomed to the basic process of pop-up card construction, you can start experimenting and create your own original designs with elements hand tailored for the special people in your life. I know how much I love sharing the cards I make with others and think you'll love this part of giving them away too! I'm grateful to share with you these easy to follow techniques and card designs.
I hope you receive much joy and satisfaction from making and sharing these artful 3D greetings with all your family and friends.

The sky's the limit, so let's get started making pop-up cards!

Before You Begin

There are no highly specialized tools or complicated techniques needed to construct these projects. Here is an overview of the basics for creating cards that really pop!

Basic Materials

Decorative paper: Use scrapbook paper, wrapping paper, and maps to add print and color to cards.

Paper doily: Use a paper doily as a decorative accent.

Craft paper: Use craft paper as the main material for pop-up cards. Look for multicolored packages at art supply, stationery, and discount stores.

Tracing paper: Use tracing paper to transfer templates and as a decorative element to add dimension to cards.

Embellishment Materials

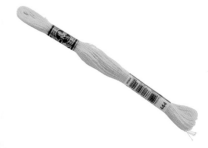

Ribbon: Use ribbon to make bows or to decorate the edges of a card.

Rhinestones and beads: Use rhinestones and beads to add texture to a card's design.

Embroidery thread: Use embroidery thread to make small bows or suspend elements from the card.

Tips for Selecting Paper

Make sure your main paper is not too thin. If the paper is too thin, the pop-up mechanism may not work. In addition, thin paper can cause wrinkles and curled edges.

The main paper should be the same color on both sides since the wrong side of the card may be visible due to the design of the pop-up mechanism.

Thinner paper works well for cutting shapes with the craft punch.

Basic Tools

Cutting mat: Use a cutting mat to protect the table and provide a non-slip work surface. Look for a self-healing mat, which remains smooth even after repeated use.

Craft knife: For best results, use a craft knife, which allows for better precision than scissors. Many craft knifes are available with interchangeable blades: use 45° angle blades for regular cutting and 30° angle blades for intricate details.

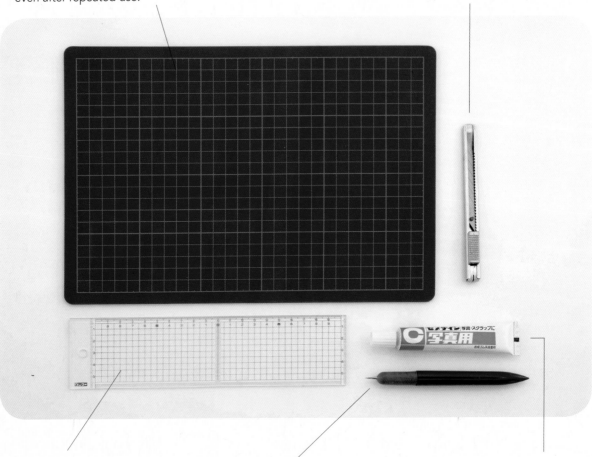

Ruler: Use a ruler as a measuring device and a straight edge cutting guide.

Stylus: Use a stylus to mark fold lines. You can make your own stylus from an old ballpoint pen, just make sure all the ink is gone first.

Glue: Use photo paper glue to prevent wrinkling the paper.

Embellishment Tools

Craft punch: Use a craft punch to cut out small shapes, such as circles, hearts, and flowers.

Masking tape: Use making tape to temporarily secure tracing paper when transferring templates. Decorative tape can also be used to embellish cards.

Pens: Use pens to personalize cards with messages and artwork. Waterproof gel pens work best.

Basic Construction Techniques

Most of the cards in this book are constructed with a basic pop-up mechanism. The following guide shows how to transfer the construction diagram to the inner card paper and create the pop-up mechanism. This guide uses the "Good Enough to Eat" card on page 26 as an example, but this basic construction technique applies to many of the cards in this book.

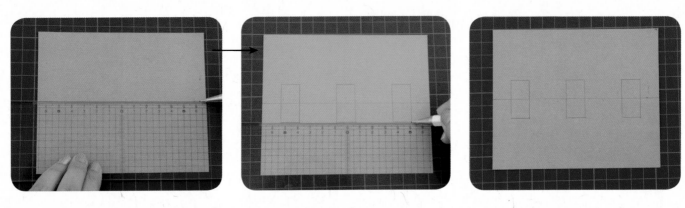

1. Cut the inner card to size according to the dimensions listed in the construction diagram. Transfer the construction diagram using a mechanical pencil and ruler. Mark the center fold first, then mark the other lines.

2. Cut along the cutting lines using a craft knife. Use a ruler as a guide to help cut smooth, straight lines.

3. Mark the fold lines using a stylus. Erase the pencil lines, being careful not to crease the paper.

4. Push out the mountain fold boxes from the wrong side.

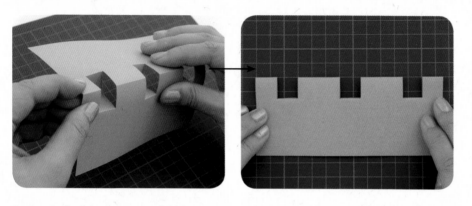

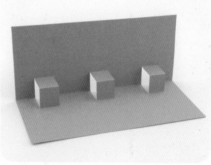

5. Once all of the mountain fold boxes have been pushed out, fold the card closed and crease the center fold line.

6. Open the card to complete the basic pop-up mechanism.

Construction Diagram

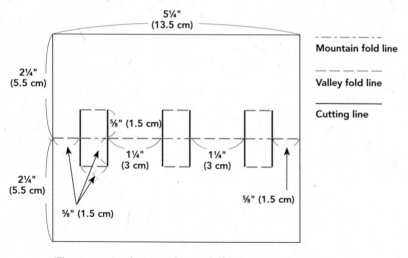

5¼"
(13.5 cm)

2¼"
(5.5 cm)

⅝" (1.5 cm)

1¼"
(3 cm)

1¼"
(3 cm)

2¼"
(5.5 cm)

⅝" (1.5 cm)

⅝" (1.5 cm)

- - - - - **Mountain fold line**

— — — — **Valley fold line**

———— **Cutting line**

*The construction diagram is shown at half-scale.

You can also transfer the construction diagram using a photocopier. Since all of the construction diagrams are half-size, enlarge the diagram 200% when photocopying. Layer the photocopy on top of the inner card paper, then follow steps 3-5.

How to Transfer the Templates

Almost all of the cards in this book are made with templates. The following guide shows how to transfer the templates to the paper you wish to use for the card. The guide uses the "Good Enough to Eat" card on page 26, but this basic technique applies throughout the book.

1. Layer the tracing paper on top of the template you wish to transfer. Trace the template outline using a mechanical pencil.

2. Layer the tracing paper with the template outline on top of the paper you wish to cut. Secure the tracing paper in place using masking tape.

3. Cut along the template outline using a craft knife. Rotate the paper as needed to allow for a smooth cutting process.

**Heart
Paper E
(cut 3)**

You can also transfer the templates using a photocopier. Simply photocopy the template and layer it on top of the paper you wish to cut, as shown at left, then cut along the template outline using a craft knife.

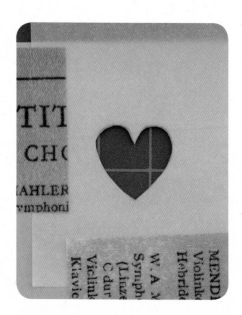

4. The template is completely cut out.

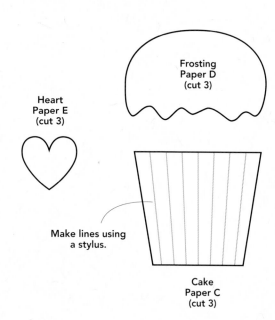

**Heart
Paper E
(cut 3)**

**Frosting
Paper D
(cut 3)**

**Make lines using
a stylus.**

**Cake
Paper C
(cut 3)**

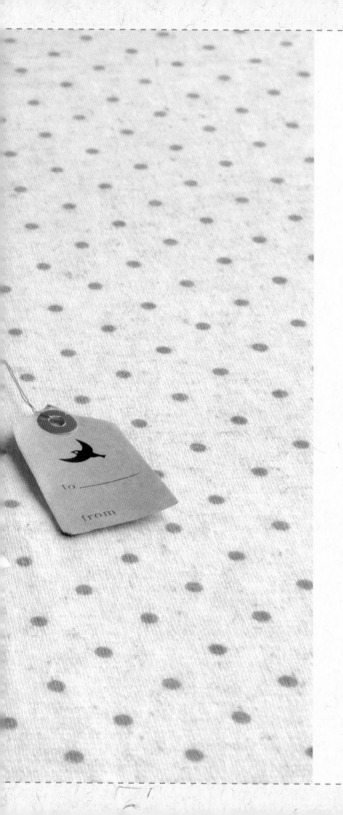

Projects

With your basic tools and techniques
ready to go, celebrate any occasion
with one of these playful cards.

Teacup Bouquet

GREAT FOR • Birthday • Thank You • Get Well Soon • Mother's Day • Blank Greeting

Materials

Paper A (red):
One 4 ¾" x 6 ¾" (12 x 17 cm) piece
Paper B (pink):
One 4" x 6" (10 x 15 cm) piece
Paper C (red):
One 2" x 3 ¼" (5 x 8 cm) piece
Paper D (white):
One 3 ¼" x 3 ¼" (8 x 8 cm) piece
Paper E (bright green):
One 1 ¼" x 3 ¼" (3 x 8 cm) piece
Paper F (yellow):
One 1 ¼" x 1 ¼" (3 x 3 cm) piece

Tools

¼" (6 mm) circle craft punch
Basic tools shown on page 10

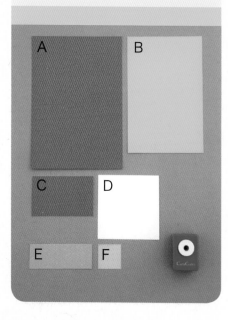

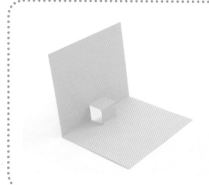

How It Works

The pop-up mechanism for this card is a convex square located at the center of Paper B.

Construction Diagram

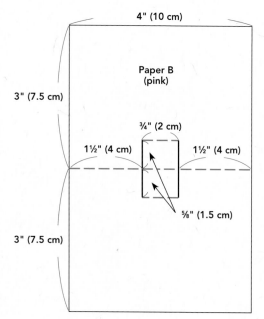

4" (10 cm)

Paper B
(pink)

3" (7.5 cm)

¾" (2 cm)

1½" (4 cm)   1½" (4 cm)

⅝" (1.5 cm)

3" (7.5 cm)

- - - · - - - · — Mountain fold line

- - - - - - · — Valley fold line

———————— Cutting line

*The construction diagram is shown at half-scale.

1. Fold Paper A in half lengthwise. Transfer the construction diagram to Paper B, then make cuts and folds as shown on page 19 (refer to page 12 for basic construction techniques).

2. Align Paper A and B at the center fold and glue together, making sure to keep the pop-up mechanism on Paper B unattached.

3. Using the templates on page 21, make one teacup of Paper C and two flowers of Paper D. Use the ¼" (6 mm) circle craft punch to make five circles of Paper D.

4. Glue the circles to the cup.

5. Using the template on page 21, make four leaves of Paper E. Use the ¼" (6 mm) circle craft punch to make two circles of Paper F. Glue a circle to the center of each flower.

6. Position the flowers and leaves along the top of the teacup, making sure the arrangement fits within the card completely, then glue.

7. Glue the finished teacup to the pop-up mechanism of Paper B to complete the card.

Full-Size Templates

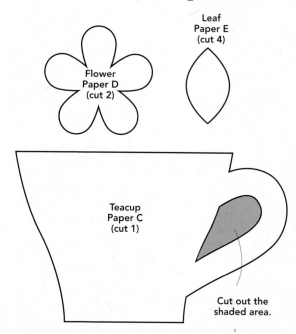

Flower
Paper D
(cut 2)

Leaf
Paper E
(cut 4)

Teacup
Paper C
(cut 1)

Cut out the
shaded area.

Close-Up View

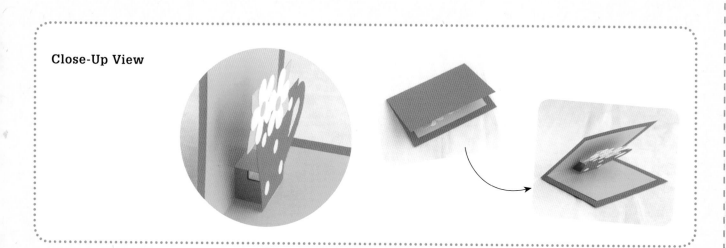

Bearing Gifts

GREAT FOR • Birthday • Thank You • Baby Shower

Materials

Paper A (dark yellow):
One 5" x 7" (12.6 x 17.6 cm) piece
Paper B (light yellow):
One 4 ¾" x 6 ¾" (12 x 17 cm) piece
Paper C (orange):
One ¼" x 2 ¾" (5 mm x 7 cm) piece
Paper D (orange):
One 1 ½" x 3 ¼" (4 x 8 cm) piece
Paper E (yellow):
One 2" x 2" (5 x 5 cm) piece
Paper F (light brown):
One 3 ¼" x 3 ½" (8 x 9 cm) piece
Paper G (white):
One 2" x 2" (5 x 5 cm) piece
Paper H (dark brown):
One 1 ¼" x 1 ¼" (3 x 3 cm) piece
Wire: One ¾" (2 cm) piece of green
28-gauge wire

Tools

⅛" (3 mm) circle craft punch
Small flower craft punch
Basic tools shown on page 10

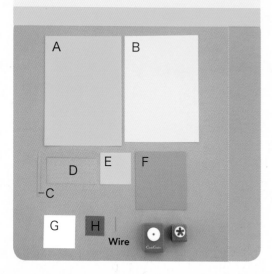

How It Works

The pop-up mechanism for this card is a convex square located on the left side of Paper B.

Construction Diagram

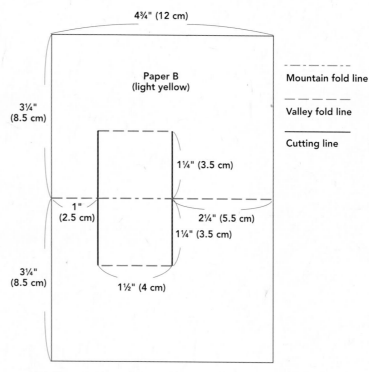

4¾" (12 cm)

Paper B
(light yellow)

3¼"
(8.5 cm)

1¼" (3.5 cm)

1"
(2.5 cm)

2¼" (5.5 cm)

1¼" (3.5 cm)

3¼"
(8.5 cm)

1½" (4 cm)

- - - - · Mountain fold line

———— Valley fold line

———— Cutting line

*The construction diagram is shown at half-scale.

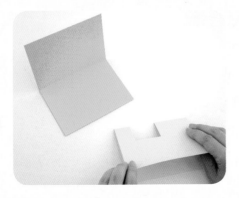

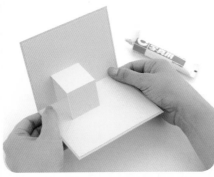

1. Fold Paper A in half lengthwise. Transfer the construction diagram to Paper B, then make cuts and folds as shown on page 23 (refer to page 12 for basic construction techniques).

2. Align Paper A and B at the center fold and glue together, making sure to keep the pop-up mechanism on Paper B unattached.

3. Fold Paper C in half lengthwise and glue to the center of the pop-up mechanism. Using the template on page 25, make one ribbon of Paper D and glue to the top of the pop-up mechanism to form the gift.

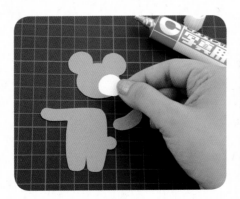

4. Using the templates on page 25, make the bear's head, body, and arm of Paper F and mouth of Paper G. Glue the mouth to the head.

5. Assemble the bear by gluing the head, body, and arm together. Use the ⅛" (3 mm) circle craft punch to make three circles of Paper H. Glue the circles to the bear to form the eyes and nose.

6. Use the small flower craft punch to make a flower of Paper F and the ⅛" (3 mm) circle craft punch to make a circle of Paper D. Glue the circle to the center of the flower. Glue the wire to the wrong side of the flower.

7. Position the flower underneath the bear's arm and glue.

8. Using the template below, make a tag of Paper G, then glue the tag to the gift. Glue the bear to Paper B at the right of the gift. Use the ⅛" (3 mm) circle craft punch to make four circles of Paper D. Glue a circle to each corner of Paper B to complete the card.

Full-Size Templates

Tag
Paper G
(cut 1)

Mouth
Paper G
(cut 1)

Area to
attach to
body

Bear
Paper F (cut 1
of each part)

Area to
attach to
head

Ribbon
Paper D
(cut 1 on fold)

Fold line

Close-Up View

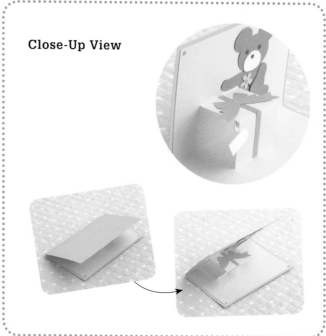

Good Enough to Eat

GREAT FOR • Birthday • Party Invitation • Thank You • Valentine's Day

Materials

Paper A (beige):
One 5 ½" x 5 ¾" (14 x 14.5 cm) piece
Paper B (yellow):
One 4 ¼" x 5 ¼" (11 x 13.5 cm) piece
Paper C (beige):
Three 1 ¼" x 1 ½" (3 x 3.5 cm) pieces
Paper D (light green, light pink, light blue):
One 1" x 2" (2.5 x 5 cm) piece each
Paper E (yellow):
One ¾" x 2 ½" (2 x 6 cm) piece
Beads:
Three 1/16" (2 mm) pearl beads in each light green, light pink, light blue

Tools

Basic tools shown on page 10

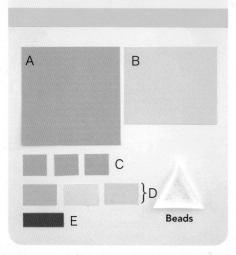

How It Works
The pop-up mechanisms for this card are three convex squares located on Paper B.

Construction Diagram

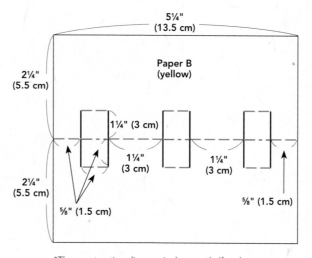

5¼"
(13.5 cm)

2¼"
(5.5 cm)

Paper B
(yellow)

2¼"
(5.5 cm)

1¼" (3 cm)

1¼"
(3 cm)

1¼"
(3 cm)

⅝" (1.5 cm)

⅝" (1.5 cm)

- - - - - Mountain fold line

———— Valley fold line

———— Cutting line

*The construction diagram is shown at half-scale.

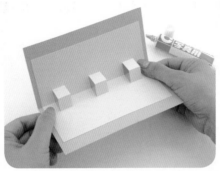

1. Fold Paper A in half lengthwise. Transfer the construction diagram to Paper B, then make cuts and folds as shown on page 27 (refer to page 12 for basic construction techniques).

2. Align Paper A and B at the center fold and glue together, making sure to keep the pop-up mechanisms on Paper B unattached.

3. Using the templates on page 29, make three cakes of Paper C. Make vertical lines on each cake using a stylus.

4. Using the templates on page 29, make three frosting pieces of Paper D and three hearts of Paper E. Glue a frosting piece and heart to each cake.

5. Glue the pearl beads to the cupcake with the corresponding color of frosting.

6. Glue the finished cupcakes to the pop-up mechanisms to complete the card.

Full-Size Templates

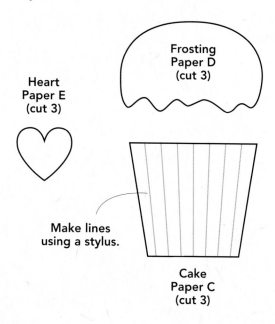

Frosting
Paper D
(cut 3)

Heart
Paper E
(cut 3)

Make lines
using a stylus.

Cake
Paper C
(cut 3)

Close-Up View

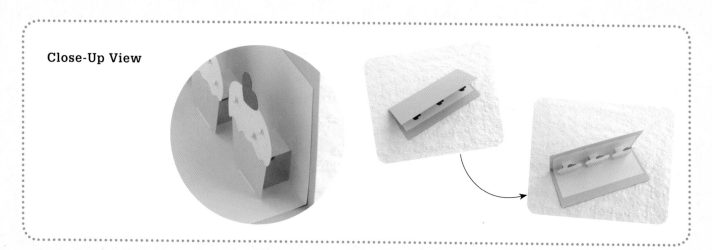

Bouquet of Balloons

GREAT FOR • Birthday • Party Invitation • Thank You • Congratulations • Blank Greeting

Materials

Paper A (bright blue):
One 5 ½" x 5 ¾" (13.6 x 14.3 cm) piece
Paper B (light blue):
One 5 ¼" x 5 ½" (13 x 14 cm) piece
Paper C (bright blue):
Six ¼" x 1 ½" (5 mm x 4 cm) pieces
Paper D (green, orange, yellow, pink, bright blue, purple):
One 1 ½" x 1 ½" (4 x 4 cm) pieces
Paper E (any color):
Two ⅜" x ⅜" (1 x 1 cm) pieces
Paper F (white):
Two ⅝" x ¾" (1.5 x 2 cm) pieces
Wire: Two 2" (5 cm) pieces of 28-gauge wire
Two 2" (5 cm) pieces of 28-gauge wire
One 2 ½" (6 cm) piece of 28-gauge wire
One 2 ¾" (7 cm) piece of 28-gauge wire
One 3 ½" (9 cm) piece of 28-gauge wire
One 4" (10 cm) piece of 28-gauge wire

Tools

Basic tools shown on page 10

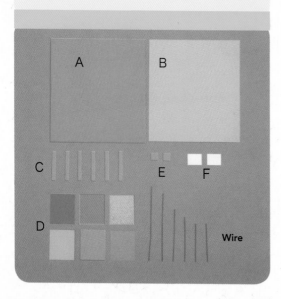

How It Works

The pop-up mechanism for this card is a convex square located the bottom of Paper B.

Construction Diagram

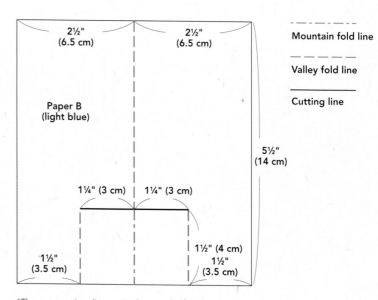

	Mountain fold line
	Valley fold line
	Cutting line

2½" (6.5 cm)   2½" (6.5 cm)

Paper B (light blue)

5½" (14 cm)

1¼" (3 cm)   1¼" (3 cm)

1½" (4 cm)

1½" (3.5 cm)   1½" (3.5 cm)

*The construction diagram is shown at half-scale.

1. Fold Paper A in half lengthwise. Transfer the construction diagram to Paper B, then make cuts and folds as shown on page 31 (refer to page 12 for basic construction techniques).

2. Evenly position the six Paper C pieces on the pop-up mechanism and glue.

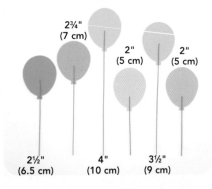

2¾"
(7 cm)

2"
(5 cm)

2"
(5 cm)

2½"
(6.5 cm)

4"
(10 cm)

3½"
(9 cm)

3. Using the template on page 33, make six balloons of Paper D. Glue the wires to the wrong side of each balloon, as shown in the photo.

4. Glue a piece of Paper F to each side of the wire on the orange balloon.

5. Insert the pink and orange balloons through the pop-up mechanism from the wrong side. To secure the balloons, glue each Paper E piece to Paper B with the wire sandwiched in between.

6. Check the right side to make sure the balloons are positioned correctly.

7. Glue the four remaining balloons to Paper B.

8. Align Paper A and B at the center fold and glue, making sure to keep the pop-up mechanism unattached. Make sure the bottoms of both Paper A and B are aligned.

Full-Size Template

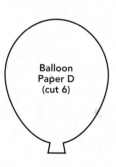

Balloon
Paper D
(cut 6)

Close-Up View

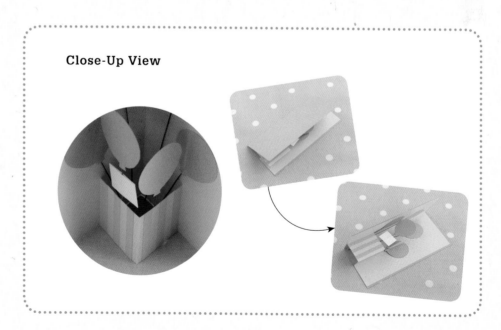

Tulips to Treasure

BIRTHDAY • Thank You • Get Well Soon • Mother's Day • Blank Greeting

Materials

Paper A (bright green):
One 3 ¾" x 8 ¼" (9.5 x 21 cm) piece
Paper B (white):
One 3 ¼" x 8" (8.5 x 20 cm) piece
Paper C (green):
One 2" x 2 ½" (5 x 6 cm) piece
Paper D (yellow):
One 2" x 4" (5 x 10 cm) piece
Paper E (bright green):
Two ¹⁄₁₆" x 2" (2 mm x 5 cm) pieces
Paper F (light green):
One 2" x 2 ½" (5 x 6 cm) piece

Tools

⅛" (3 mm) circle craft punch
Basic tools shown on page 10

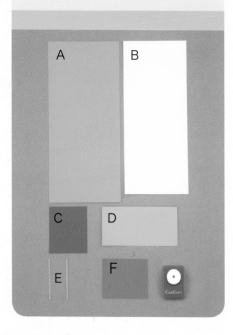

How It Works

The pop-up mechanism for this card is a convex rectangle located at the center of Paper B.

Construction Diagram

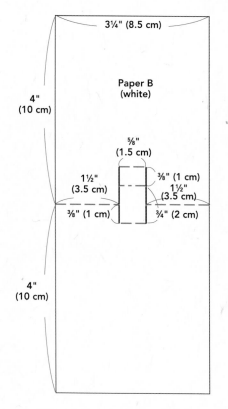

3¼" (8.5 cm)

Paper B
(white)

4"
(10 cm)

⅝"
(1.5 cm)

1½"
(3.5 cm)

⅜" (1 cm)
1½"
(3.5 cm)

⅜" (1 cm)

¾" (2 cm)

4"
(10 cm)

– – – Mountain fold line

– – – – Valley fold line

——— Cutting line

*The construction diagram is shown at half-scale.

35

1. Fold Paper A in half lengthwise. Transfer the construction diagram to Paper B, then make cuts and folds as shown on page 35 (refer to page 12 for basic construction techniques).

2. Align Paper A and B at the center fold and glue together, making sure to keep the pop-up mechanism on Paper B unattached.

3. Using the templates on page 37, make one vase of Paper C, two Tulip A pieces of Paper D, two Tulip B pieces of Paper D, one bow of Paper D, and four leaves of Paper F.

4. Glue each Tulip A piece on top of a Tulip B piece. Glue each tulip to a Paper E piece.

5. Position the flowers and leaves at the top of the vase, making sure the arrangement is less than 3 ¾" (9.5 cm) tall. Glue the flowers and leaves to the wrong side of the vase. Glue the bow to the right side of the vase.

6. Glue the finished vase to the pop-up mechanism. Use the ⅛" (3 mm) circle craft punch to make four circles of Paper F. Glue a circle to each corner of Paper B to complete the card.

Full-Size Templates

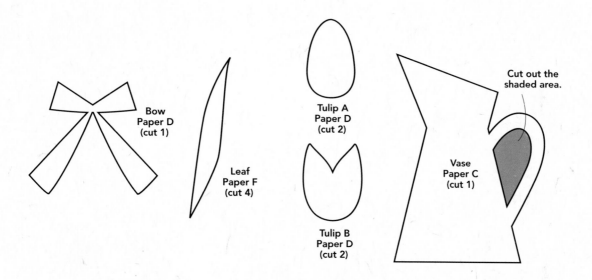

Bow
Paper D
(cut 1)

Leaf
Paper F
(cut 4)

Tulip A
Paper D
(cut 2)

Tulip B
Paper D
(cut 2)

Vase
Paper C
(cut 1)

Cut out the
shaded area.

Close-Up View

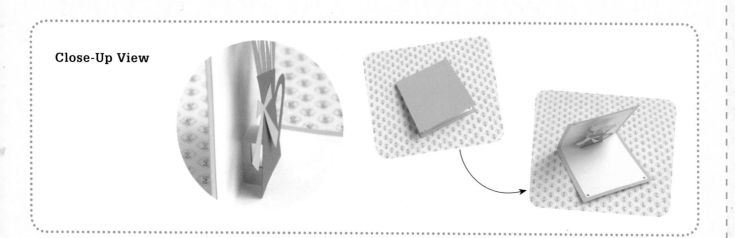

Snowman Greetings

GREAT FOR • Holiday/Christmas • Party Invitation

Materials

Paper A (dark blue):
One 5 ¼" x 7" (13.6 x 17.6 cm) piece

Paper B (light blue):
One 5" x 6 ¾" (13 x 17 cm) piece

Paper C (white):
One 2 ½" x 2 ½" (6 x 6 cm) piece

Paper D (red):
One 1 ½" x 1 ½" (4 x 4 cm) piece

Paper E (dark blue):
One 1 ¼" x 1 ¼" (3 x 3 cm) piece

Paper F (light pink):
One 1 ¼" x 1 ¼" (3 x 3 cm) piece

Paper G (green):
One 2" x 4 ¾" (5 x 12 cm) piece

Paper H (light green):
One 2" x 2 ½" (5 x 6 cm) piece

Paper I (yellow):
One ¾" x ¾" (2 x 2 cm) piece

Tools

⅛" (3 mm) circle craft punch
³⁄₁₆" (5 mm) circle craft punch
Basic tools shown on page 10

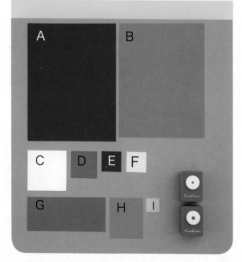

How It Works
The pop-up mechanisms for this card are two convex rectangles located on Paper B.

Construction Diagram

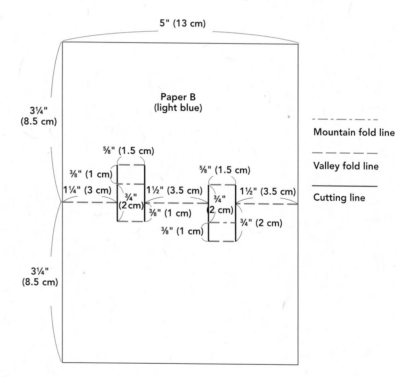

5" (13 cm)

3¼" (8.5 cm)

Paper B (light blue)

⅝" (1.5 cm)

⅜" (1 cm)

1¼" (3 cm)

¾" (2 cm)

1½" (3.5 cm)

⅜" (1 cm)

⅝" (1.5 cm)

¾" (2 cm)

1½" (3.5 cm)

⅜" (1 cm)

¾" (2 cm)

3¼" (8.5 cm)

– – – – – Mountain fold line

———— Valley fold line

———— Cutting line

*The construction diagram is shown at half-scale.

 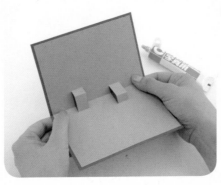 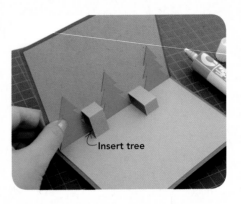

1. Fold Paper A in half lengthwise. Transfer the construction diagram to Paper B, then make cuts and folds as shown on page 39 (refer to page 12 for basic construction techniques).

2. Align Paper A and B at the center fold and glue together, making sure to keep the pop-up mechanisms on Paper B unattached.

3. Using the templates on page 41, make three small trees of Paper G. Glue the trees to the background of Paper B. Note that the bottom of one of the trees should be inserted behind the left pop-up mechanism.

 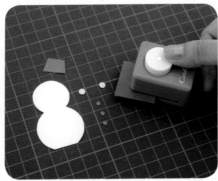 

4. Using the templates on page 41, make one large tree of Paper H and one star of Paper I. Glue the star to the top of the large tree, then glue the tree to the left pop-up mechanism.

5. Using the templates on page 41, make one snowman of Paper C and one hat of Paper D. Use the ⅛" (3 mm) circle craft punch to make three circles of Paper D and two circles of Paper E. Use the ³⁄₁₆" (5 mm) circle craft punch to make two circles of Paper F.

6. Glue the circles to the snowman to form the eyes, cheeks, and buttons. Glue the hat to the snowman's head. Glue the finished snowman to the right pop-up mechanism.

7. Use the ⅛" (3 mm) circle craft punch to make seven circles of Paper C. Glue the circles to the background of Paper B to complete the card.

Full-Size Templates

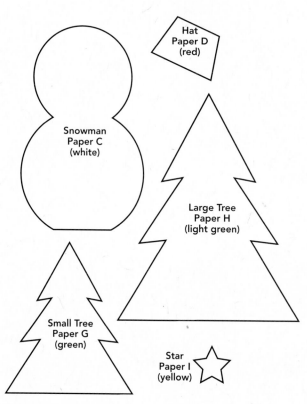

Hat
Paper D
(red)

Snowman
Paper C
(white)

Large Tree
Paper H
(light green)

Small Tree
Paper G
(green)

Star
Paper I
(yellow)

Close-Up View

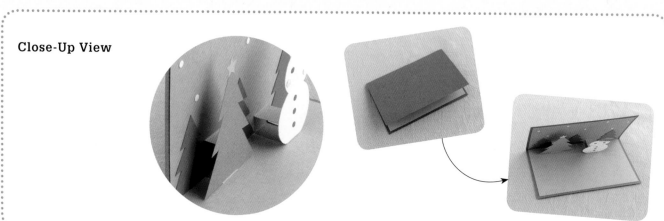

All Wrapped Up

GREAT FOR • Birthday • Thank You • Get Well Soon • Mother's Day • Blank Greeting

Materials

Paper A (white):
One 5" x 6 ¼" (12.6 x 15.6 cm) piece

Paper B (bright green):
One 4 ¾" x 6" (12 x 15 cm) piece

Paper C (green):
One 2 ¾" x 2 ¾" (7 x 7 cm) piece

Paper D (white):
One 2" x 2" (5 x 5 cm) piece

Paper E (bright blue):
One 1 ¼" x 3 ¼" (3 x 8 cm) piece

Paper F (yellow)
One 2" x 2" (5 x 5 cm) piece

Tools

⅛" (3 mm) circle craft punch
Small daisy craft punch
Basic tools shown on page 10

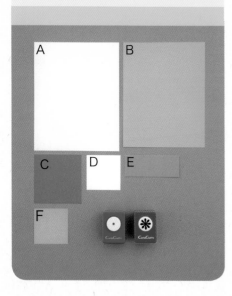

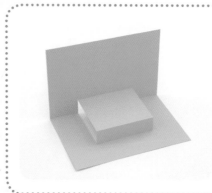

How It Works

The pop-up mechanism for this card is a convex rectangle located at the center of Paper B.

Construction Diagram

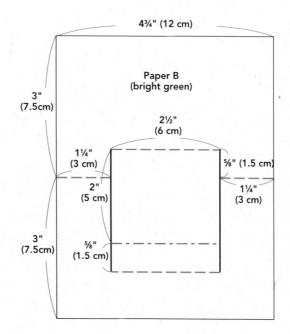

4¾" (12 cm)

Paper B (bright green)

3" (7.5cm)

2½" (6 cm)

1¼" (3 cm)

⅝" (1.5 cm)

2" (5 cm)

1¼" (3 cm)

3" (7.5cm)

⅝" (1.5 cm)

- - - - - Mountain fold line

– – – – – Valley fold line

——— Cutting line

*The construction diagram is shown at half-scale.

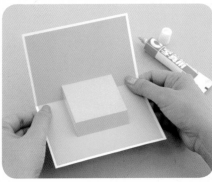

1. Fold Paper A in half lengthwise. Transfer the construction diagram to Paper B, then make cuts and folds as shown on page 43 (refer to page 12 for basic construction techniques).

2. Align Paper A and B at the center fold and glue together, making sure to keep the pop-up mechanism on Paper B unattached.

3. Use the small daisy craft punch to make five daisies of Paper D. Use the ⅛" (3 mm) circle craft punch to make five circles of Paper F. Glue a circle to the center of each daisy.

4. Using the templates on page 45, make one Ribbon A, one Ribbon B, one Ribbon C, and four stems.

5. Glue a daisy to each stem. Glue the finished daisies to the background of Paper B.

6. Glue Ribbons A, B, and C to the pop-up mechanism. Glue the remaining daisy to the center of Ribbon A.

7. Using the templates below, make two birds of Paper E and one envelope of Paper C. Make a valley fold along the envelope fold line to form the flap, then glue the flap down.

8. Glue the birds and envelope to Paper B. Use the ⅛" (3 mm) circle craft punch to make four circles of Paper C. Glue a circle to each corner of Paper B to complete the card.

Full-Size Templates

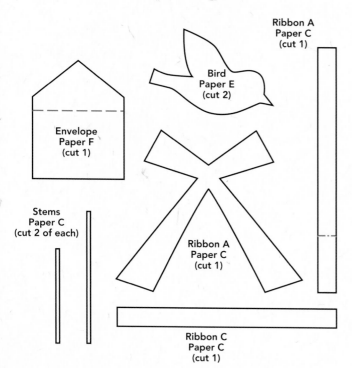

Envelope
Paper F
(cut 1)

Stems
Paper C
(cut 2 of each)

Bird
Paper E
(cut 2)

Ribbon A
Paper C
(cut 1)

Ribbon A
Paper C
(cut 1)

Ribbon C
Paper C
(cut 1)

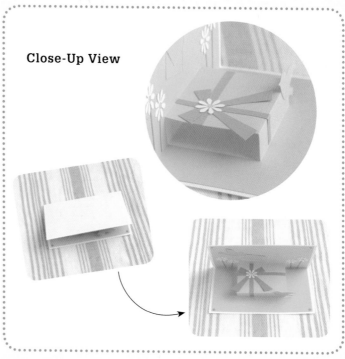

Close-Up View

Up, Up, and Away

GREAT FOR • Bon Voyage • Party Invitation • Thank You • Blank Greeting

Materials

Paper A (bright blue):
One 5" x 7" (12.3 x 17.6 cm) piece
Paper B (light blue):
One 4 ¾" x 6 ¾" (12 x 17 cm) piece
Paper C (yellow):
One 4" x 4" (10 x 10 cm) piece
Paper D (orange):
One 2 ½" x 4" (6 x 10 cm) piece
Paper E (white):
One 2" x 2" (5 x 5 cm) piece
Paper F (light green):
One 1 ¼" x 3 ¼" (3 x 8 cm) piece
Embroidery thread:
One 4 ¾" (12 cm) piece of yellow
embroidery thread

Tools

Basic tools shown on page 10

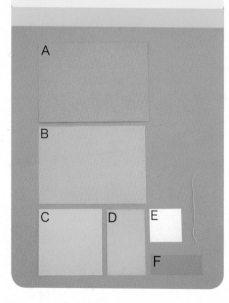

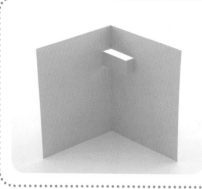

How It Works

The pop-up mechanism for this card is a convex rectangle located at the top of Paper B.

Construction Diagram

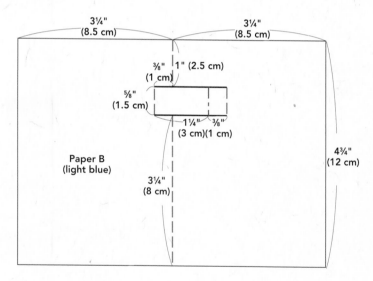

3¼"
(8.5 cm)

3¼"
(8.5 cm)

⅜"
(1 cm)

1" (2.5 cm)

⅝"
(1.5 cm)

1¼"   ⅜"
(3 cm)(1 cm)

Paper B
(light blue)

3¼"
(8 cm)

4¾"
(12 cm)

*The construction diagram is shown at half-scale.

- - - - - Mountain fold line

– – – – Valley fold line

———— Cutting line

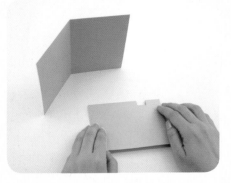

1. Fold Paper A in half widthwise. Transfer the construction diagram to Paper B, then make cuts and folds as shown on page 47 (refer to page 12 for basic construction techniques).

2. Align Paper A and B at the center fold and glue, making sure to keep the pop-up mechanism unattached. Make sure the bottoms of both Paper A and B are aligned.

3. Using the templates on page 49, make one balloon of Paper C, three stripes of Paper D, and one basket of Paper D. Glue the stripes to the balloon.

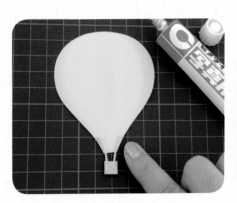

4. Cut the embroidery thread into two ¾" (2 cm) pieces and one 3 ¼" (8 cm) piece. Glue each ¾" (2 cm) piece to the wrong side of the balloon and basket to connect.

5. Tie the 3 ¼" (8 cm) piece of embroidery thread in a bow. Glue the bow to the basket.

6. Using the templates on page 49, make three birds of Paper C, two clouds of Paper E, and the left and right mountains of Paper F.

7. Glue one cloud to the balloon. Glue the finished balloon to the pop-up mechanism.

8. Glue the remaining cloud, birds, and mountains to Paper B to complete the card.

Full-Size Templates

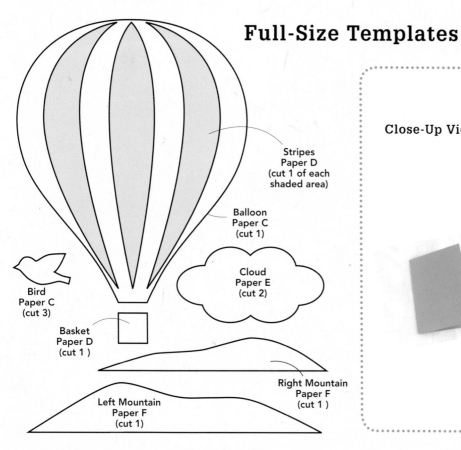

Stripes
Paper D
(cut 1 of each
shaded area)

Balloon
Paper C
(cut 1)

Cloud
Paper E
(cut 2)

Bird
Paper C
(cut 3)

Basket
Paper D
(cut 1)

Right Mountain
Paper F
(cut 1)

Left Mountain
Paper F
(cut 1)

Close-Up View

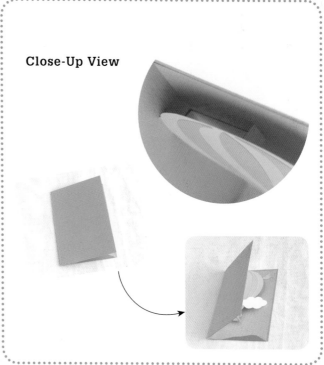

Halloween Fun

GREAT FOR • Party Invitation • Halloween Greetings

Materials

Paper A (navy blue):
One 5 ¼" x 5 ¾" (13 x 14.4 cm) piece
Paper B (dark blue):
One 5" x 5 ½" (12.5 x 15 cm) piece
Paper C (orange):
One 2 ½" x 2 ¾" (6 x 7 cm) piece
Paper D (white):
One 2" x 2 ½" (5 x 6 cm) piece
Paper E (black):
One 2 ¾" x 2 ¾" (7 x 7 cm) piece
Paper F (yellow):
Two 1 ½" x 1 ½" (4 x 4 cm) pieces
Rhinestones:
Two ⅛" (3 mm) round rhinestones in black
Seven ⅛" (3 mm) star-shaped rhinestones in silver

Tools

Basic tools shown on page 10

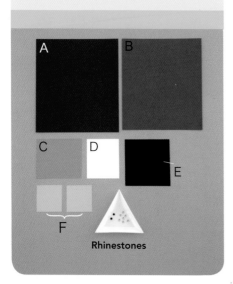

A B

C D

E

F

Rhinestones

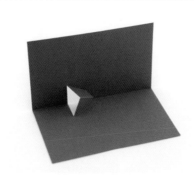

How It Works

The pop-up mechanism for this card is a convex trapezoid located on the left side of Paper B.

Full-Size Templates

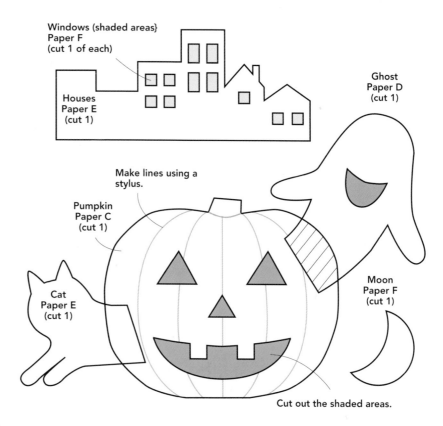

Windows (shaded areas)
Paper F
(cut 1 of each)

Houses
Paper E
(cut 1)

Ghost
Paper D
(cut 1)

Make lines using a stylus.

Pumpkin
Paper C
(cut 1)

Cat
Paper E
(cut 1)

Moon
Paper F
(cut 1)

Cut out the shaded areas.

 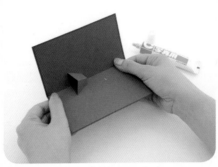 

1. Fold Paper A in half lengthwise. Transfer the construction diagram to Paper B, then make cuts and folds as shown on page 53 (refer to page 12 for basic construction techniques).

2. Align Paper A and B at the center fold and glue together, making sure to keep the pop-up mechanism unattached.

3. Using the templates on page 51, make a moon and eleven windows of Paper F and the houses of Paper E. Glue the windows to the houses.

4. Glue the houses and moon to the background of Paper B.

5. Using the template on page 51, make one pumpkin of Paper C. Make vertical lines on the pumpkin using a stylus.

6. Glue the remaining piece of Paper F to the wrong side of the pumpkin.

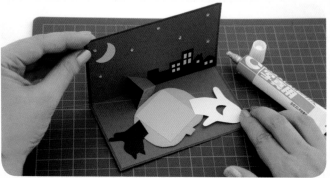

7. Using the templates on page 51, make one cat of Paper E and one ghost of Paper D. Glue the round black rhinestones to the ghost to form the eyes. Glue the ghost and cat to the wrong side of the pumpkin.

8. Glue the star-shaped silver rhinestones to the background of Paper B. Close the card slightly, then glue the finished pumpkin to the pop-up mechanism of Paper B to complete the card.

Construction Diagram

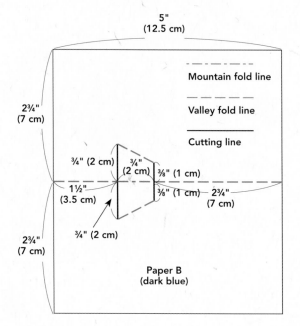

5"
(12.5 cm)

2¾"
(7 cm)

- - - - - · **Mountain fold line**

- - - - - **Valley fold line**

———— **Cutting line**

¾" (2 cm) ¾" (2 cm) ⅜" (1 cm)

1½" (3.5 cm) ⅜" (1 cm) 2¾" (7 cm)

¾" (2 cm)

2¾"
(7 cm)

Paper B
(dark blue)

*The construction diagram is shown at half-scale.

Close-Up View

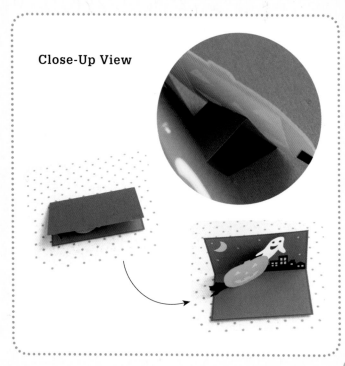

Spring Salutations

GREAT FOR • Easter • Spring Party Invitation • Thank You • Blank Greeting

Materials

Paper A (light pink):
One 5" x 6 ½" (12.5 x 16.6 cm) piece

Paper B (pink):
One 4 ¾" x 6 ¼" (12 x 16 cm) piece

Paper C (white):
One 3 ¼" x 4" (8 x 10 cm) piece

Paper D (beige):
One 1 ¼" x 1 ¼" (3 x 3 cm) piece

Paper E (light blue):
One 1 ¼" x 2 ½" (3 x 6 cm) piece

Paper F (purple):
One 2" x 4" (5 x 10 cm) piece

Wire:
One 1 ¼" (3 cm) piece of 28-gauge wire

Tools

⅛" (3 mm) circle craft punch
Small flower craft punch
Basic tools shown on page 10

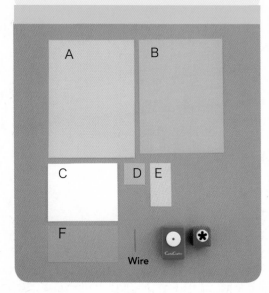

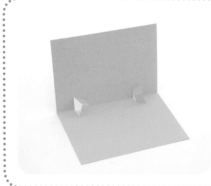

How It Works

The pop-up mechanisms for this card are two convex trapezoids located on Paper B.

Construction Diagram

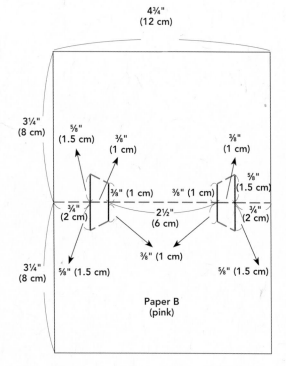

4¾"
(12 cm)

3¼"
(8 cm)

⅝"
(1.5 cm)

⅜"
(1 cm)

⅜"
(1 cm)

⅝"
(1.5 cm)

⅜" (1 cm)   ⅜" (1 cm)

¾"
(2 cm)

2½"
(6 cm)

¾"
(2 cm)

3¼"
(8 cm)

⅝" (1.5 cm)

⅜" (1 cm)

⅝" (1.5 cm)

Paper B
(pink)

– – – – – Mountain fold line

— — — Valley fold line

———— Cutting line

*The construction diagram is shown at half-scale.

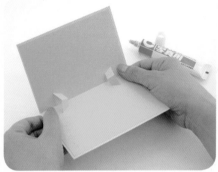

1. Fold Paper A in half lengthwise. Transfer the construction diagram to Paper B, then make cuts and folds as shown on page 55 (refer to page 12 for basic construction techniques).

2. Align Paper A and B at the center fold and glue together, making sure to keep the pop-up mechanisms unattached.

3. Use the small flower craft punch to make seven flowers of Paper E and the ⅛" (3 mm) circle craft punch to make seven circles of Paper F. Glue a circle to the center of each flower.

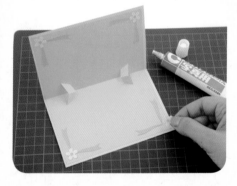

4. Using the template on page 57, make one basket of Paper D. Glue two of the flowers to the basket. Glue the wire to the wrong side of another flower.

5. Using the templates on page 57, make two rabbits and two arms of Paper C. Glue an arm to each rabbit, making sure to position the rabbits so they are facing each other. Glue the basket between the paws of one rabbit and the flower with the stem between the paws of the other rabbit.

6. Using the templates on page 57, make four of each ribbon of Paper F. Glue a set of ribbons to each corner of Paper B. Glue the four remaining flowers to each ribbon set at the corners.

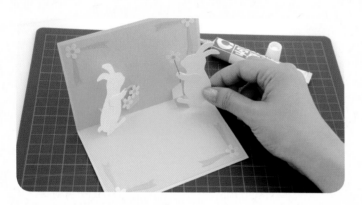

7. Glue the finished rabbits to the pop-up mechanisms of Paper B to complete the card.

Full-Size Templates

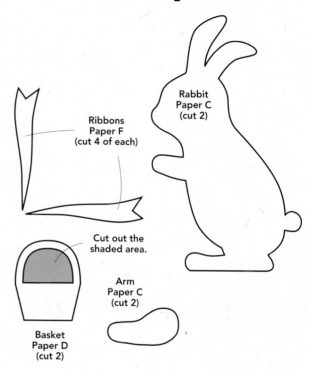

Ribbons
Paper F
(cut 4 of each)

Cut out the
shaded area.

Rabbit
Paper C
(cut 2)

Basket
Paper D
(cut 2)

Arm
Paper C
(cut 2)

Close-Up View

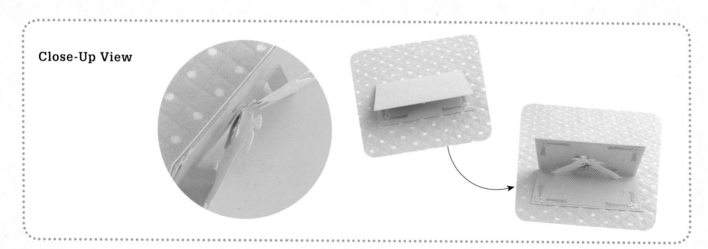

Sea View for You

GREAT FOR • Bon Voyage • Father's Day • Blank Greeting

Materials

Paper A (white):
One 5 ¼" x 5 ¾" (13 x 14.6 cm) piece
Paper B (light blue):
One 5" x 5 ½" (12.5 x 14 cm) piece
Paper C (white):
One 3 ¼" x 3 ¼" (8 x 8 cm) piece
Paper D (dark blue):
One 2" x 3 ¼" (5 x 8 cm) piece
Paper E (red):
One ⅜" x ⅝" (1 x 1.5 cm) piece
Rhinestones:
Six ⅛" (4 mm) round rhinestones in light blue
Seven ¹⁄₁₆" x ¼" (2 x 5 mm) rectangular rhinestones in dark blue
Beads:
Seven ¹⁄₁₆" (2 mm) round pearl beads in light blue
One ⅛" (3 mm) heart-shaped bead in light blue

Tools

Basic tools shown on page 10

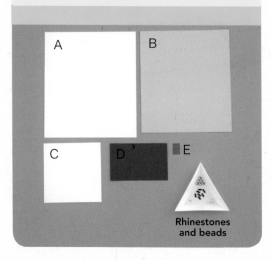

A B

C D E

Rhinestones and beads

How It Works

The pop-up mechanism for this card is a convex triangle located on the left side of Paper B.

Construction Diagram

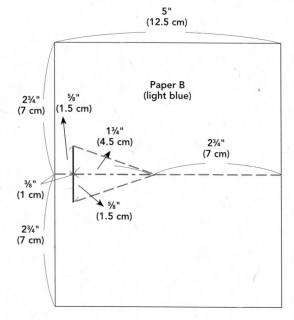

5"
(12.5 cm)

2¾"
(7 cm)

⅝"
(1.5 cm)

Paper B
(light blue)

1¾"
(4.5 cm)

2¾"
(7 cm)

⅜"
(1 cm)

⅝"
(1.5 cm)

2¾"
(7 cm)

– · – · – Mountain fold line

– – – – Valley fold line

——— Cutting line

*The construction diagram is shown at half-scale.

59

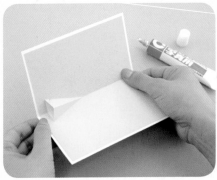

1. Fold Paper A in half lengthwise. Transfer the construction diagram to Paper B, then make cuts and folds as shown on page 59 (refer to page 12 for basic construction techniques).

2. Align Paper A and B at the center fold and glue together, making sure to keep the pop-up mechanism unattached.

3. Using the template on page 61, make one ship top of Paper C. Make the horizontal line using a stylus. Glue the rhinestones to the ship top to form the windows.

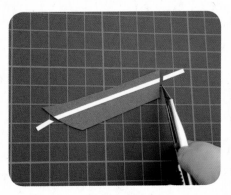

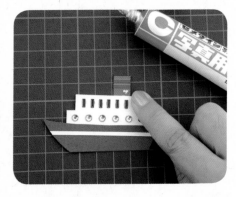

4. Using the templates on page 61, make one ship bottom of Paper D and one stripe of Paper C. Glue the strip to the ship bottom and trim the excess length.

5. Make two 1/16" x 3/8" (2 mm x 1 cm) pieces of Paper D and glue them to the top of Paper E to form the chimney.

6. Glue the ship bottom, top, and chimney together. Glue the heart-shaped bead to the chimney.

7. Using the templates below, make one cloud of Paper C and two seagulls and three fish of Paper D. Glue the cloud to the background of Paper B, about ¾" (2 cm) above the center fold. Glue the seagulls to the background and the fish to the foreground of Paper B. Glue the round pearl beads to Paper B above the fish to form bubbles.

8. Glue the finished ship to the pop-up mechanism of Paper B to complete the card.

Full-Size Templates

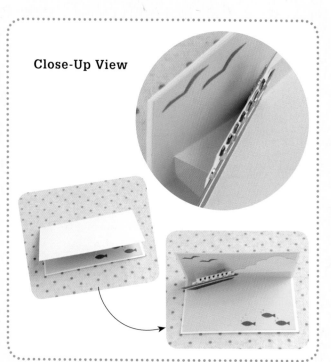

Close-Up View

Make a line using a stylus.

Ship Top
Paper C
(cut 1)

Seagull
Paper D
(cut 2)

Stripe
Paper C
(cut 1 slightly longer than the template)

Fish
Paper D
(cut 3)

Ship Bottom
Paper D
(cut 1)

Cloud
Paper C
(cut 1)

Christmas Tree Tidings

GREAT FOR • Holiday/Christmas • Party Invitation

Materials

Paper A (bright blue):
One 5 ¼" x 6 ½" (12.8 x 16.6 cm) piece
Paper B (dark blue):
One 5" x 6 ¼" (12.5 x 16 cm) piece
Paper C (bright blue):
One 3 ¼" x 3 ¼" (8 x 8 cm) piece
Paper D (white):
One 2" x 2" (5 x 5 cm) piece
Paper E (purple):
One 2" x 2" (5 x 5 cm) piece
Paper F (blue):
One 2" x 2" (5 x 5 cm) piece
Beads: Six ⅛" (3 mm) round pearl beads
in light blue
Two ¹⁄₁₆" (1.5 mm) round pearl beads
in light blue

Tools

Shining star craft punch (with small
and large star)
⅛" (3 mm) circle craft punch
³⁄₁₆" (5 mm) circle craft punch
¼" (6 mm) circle craft punch
Pen: White gel pen
Basic tools shown on page 10

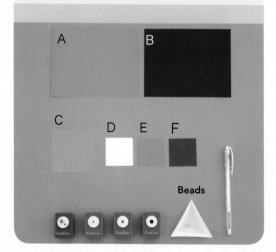

How It Works
The pop-up mechanism
for this card is a convex
triangle located at the
center of Paper B.

Construction Diagram

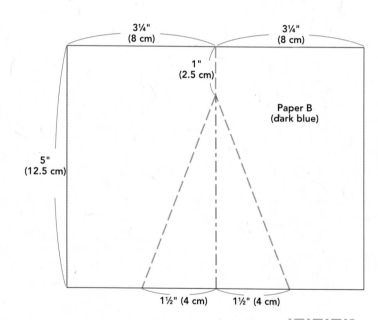

3¼"
(8 cm)

3¼"
(8 cm)

1"
(2.5 cm)

Paper B
(dark blue)

5"
(12.5 cm)

1½" (4 cm)   1½" (4 cm)

*The construction diagram is shown at half-scale.

- - - - Mountain fold line

—— · —— Valley fold line

———— Cutting line

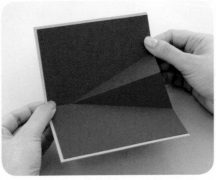

1. Fold Paper A in half lengthwise. Transfer the construction diagram to Paper B, then make cuts and folds as shown on page 63 (refer to page 12 for basic construction techniques).

2. Align Paper A and B at the center fold and glue together, making sure to keep the pop-up mechanism unattached. Make sure the bottoms of both Paper A and B are aligned.

3. Using the template on page 65, make two trees of Paper C. Use the ⅛" (3 mm) circle craft punch to make twelve circles of Paper F. Glue six circles to each tree.

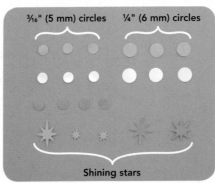

4. Glue the finished trees to Paper B.

5. Use the ³⁄₁₆" (5 mm) circle craft punch to make three circles of Paper C, three circles of Paper D, and four circles of Paper E. Use the ¼" (6 mm) circle craft punch to make three circles of Paper C and three circles of Paper D. Use the shining star craft punch to make two small stars and one large star of Paper C and two large stars of Paper E.

6. Glue the two small stars of Paper C to the two large stars of Paper E. Glue a ¹⁄₁₆" (1.5 mm) round pearl bead to the center of each star. Glue these finished stars to the top of each tree of Paper C. Glue the large star of Paper C to the top of the pop-up tree.

7. Glue the ³⁄₁₆" (5 mm) and ¼" (6 mm) circles and the six ⅛" (3 mm) round pearl beads to the pop-up tree.

8. Use a white gel pen to draw snowflakes on the background of Paper B to complete the card.

Full-Size Template

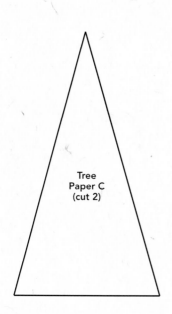

Tree
Paper C
(cut 2)

Close-Up View

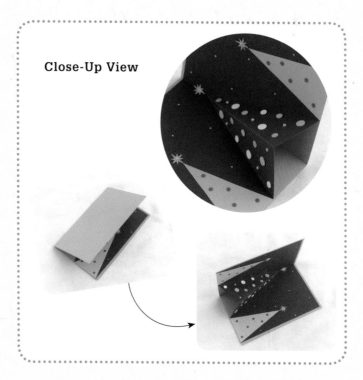

Fan with Cherry Blossoms

GREAT FOR • Thank You • Blank Greeting

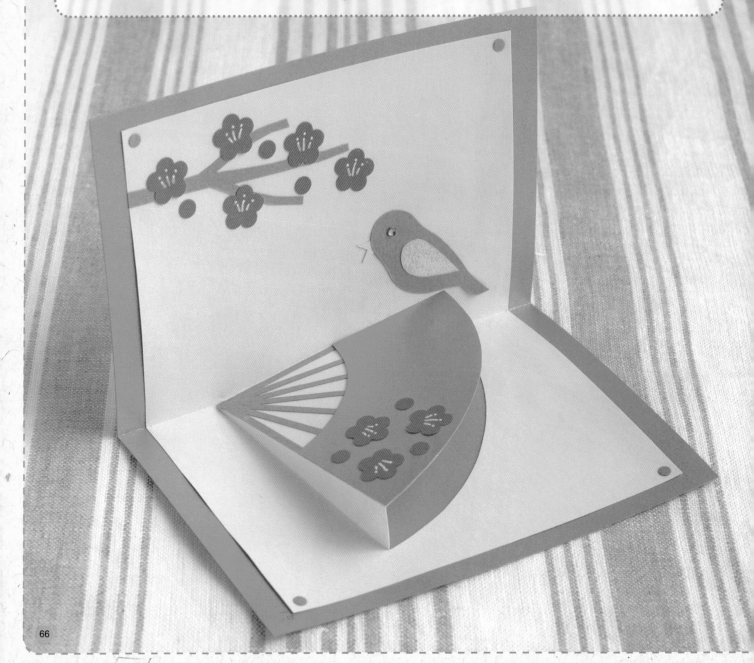

Materials

Paper A (gold):
One 5" x 6 ¾" (12.5 x 17 cm) piece
Paper B (cream):
One 4 ¼" x 6 ¼" (11 x 16 cm) piece
Paper C (gold):
One 2 ¾" x 2 ¾" (7 x7 cm) piece
Paper D (brown):
One 2" x 2 ¾" (5 x 7 cm) piece
Paper E (red):
One 2" x 2 ¾" (5 x 7 cm) piece
Paper F (yellow):
One 1" x 1" (2.5 x 2.5 cm) piece
Paper G (green):
One 1 ½" x 1 ½" (4 x 4 cm) piece
Rhinestone: One ⅛" (3 mm) round
rhinestone in orange

Tools

⅛" (3 mm) circle craft punch
³⁄₁₆" (5 mm) circle craft punch
Small cherry blossom craft punch
Pen: White gel pen
Basic tools shown on page 10

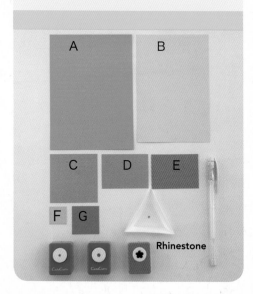

How It Works
The pop-up mechanism
for this card is a convex
fan located on Paper B.

Construction Diagram

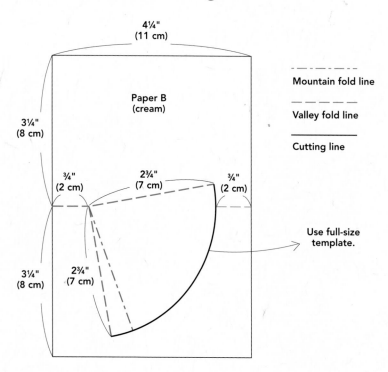

4¼"
(11 cm)

Paper B
(cream)

3¼"
(8 cm)

¾"
(2 cm)

2¾"
(7 cm)

¾"
(2 cm)

3¼"
(8 cm)

2¾"
(7 cm)

- - - - - Mountain fold line

- - - - - Valley fold line

———— Cutting line

Use full-size
template.

*The construction diagram is shown at half-scale.

1. Fold Paper A in half lengthwise. Transfer the construction diagram to Paper B, then make cuts and folds as shown on page 67 (refer to page 12 for basic construction techniques). For the pop-up mechanism, use the fan template to transfer the lines, then make cuts and folds.

2. Align Paper A and B at the center fold and glue together, making sure to keep the pop-up mechanism unattached.

3. Make seven 1/16" x 1 1/2" (2 mm x 4 cm) strips of Paper D and glue them to the top of the pop-up mechanism of Paper B in a radial pattern. Using the template on page 69, make one fan of Paper C. Glue the fan to the pop-up mechanism of Paper B along the curve.

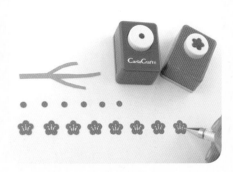

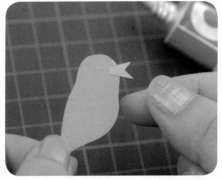

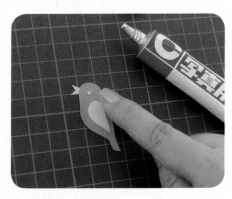

4. Using the template on page 69, make one tree branch of Paper D. Use the small cherry blossom craft punch to make eight flowers of Paper E and the 3/16" (5 mm) circle craft punch to make six circles of Paper E. Use the white gel pen to decorate the flowers.

5. Using the templates on page 69, make one bird of Paper G and one wing and one beak of Paper F. Glue the beak to the wrong side of the bird near the edge.

7. Glue the wing and the rhinestone to the bird.

7. Glue the tree branch to the background of Paper B. Glue the flowers and the ³⁄₁₆″ (5 mm) circles to both the tree branch and the fan.

8. Glue the bird to the background of Paper B at the right edge of the fan. Use the ⅛″ (3 mm) circle craft punch to make four circles of Paper C. Glue a circle to each corner of Paper B to complete the card.

Full-Size Templates

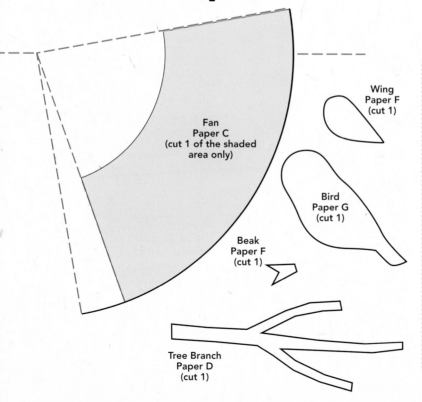

Fan
Paper C
(cut 1 of the shaded area only)

Wing
Paper F
(cut 1)

Bird
Paper G
(cut 1)

Beak
Paper F
(cut 1)

Tree Branch
Paper D
(cut 1)

Close-Up View

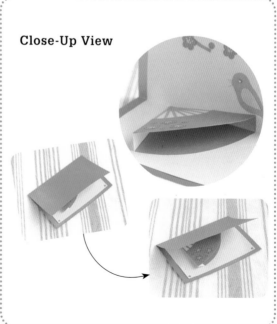

Flowers & Butterflies

GREAT FOR • Birthday • Party Invitation • Thank You • Blank Greeting

Materials

Paper A (medium pink):
One 5" x 6 ¼" (12.5 x 16 cm) piece
Paper B (white):
One 4 ½" x 6" (11.5 x 15 cm) piece
Paper C (pink vellum):
One 2 ¾" x 3 ¼" (7 x 8 cm) piece
Paper D (pink):
One 4" x 4" (10 x 10 cm) piece
Paper E (light pink):
One 2 ¾" x 2 ¾" (7 x 7 cm) piece
Paper F (light yellow)
One 2" x 2" (5 x 5 cm) piece
Paper G (light green):
One 1 ¼" x 3 ¼" (3 x 8 cm) piece
Beads:
Seven ⅛" (2.5 mm) round pearl beads in pink
Eight ¹⁄₁₆" (1.5 mm) round pearl beads in pink

Tools

Small flower craft punch
⅛" (3 mm) circle craft punch
Large flower craft punch
Basic tools shown on page 10

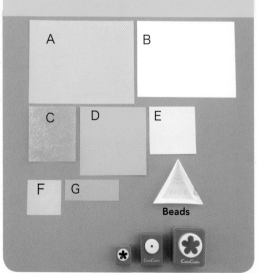

How It Works

The pop-up mechanism for this card is a convex fan located on Paper B.

Construction Diagram

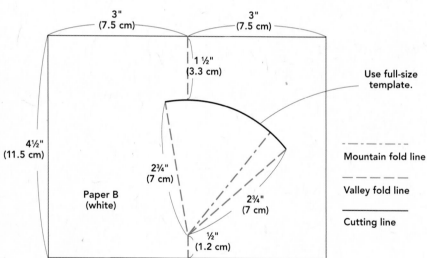

3"
(7.5 cm)

3"
(7.5 cm)

1 ½"
(3.3 cm)

Use full-size template.

4½"
(11.5 cm)

2¾"
(7 cm)

2¾"
(7 cm)

Paper B
(white)

½"
(1.2 cm)

‑ ‑ ‑ Mountain fold line

— ‑ — Valley fold line

—— Cutting line

*The construction diagram is shown at half-scale.

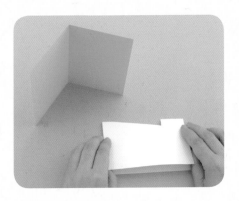

1. Fold Paper A in half widthwise. Transfer the construction diagram to Paper B, then make cuts and folds as shown on page 71 (refer to page 12 for basic construction techniques). For the pop-up mechanism, use the bouquet paper template to transfer the lines, then make cuts and folds.

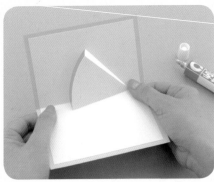

2. Align Paper A and B at the center fold and glue together, making sure to keep the pop-up mechanism unattached.

3. Using the template on page 73, make one bouquet paper of Paper C. Glue the bouquet paper to the pop-up mechanism of Paper B along the curve.

4. Using the templates on page 73, make a bow and two ribbons of Paper D. Glue the ribbons to Paper B at the bottom edge of the bouquet, then glue the bow on top.

5. Use the large flower craft punch to make four large flowers of Paper D and the small flower craft punch to make four small flowers of Paper F. Glue a small flower to the center of each large flower. Glue a 1/8" (2.5 mm) round pearl bead to the center of each flower.

6. Use the large flower craft punch to make three large flowers of Paper E and the small flower craft punch to make three small flowers of Paper D. Glue a small flower to the center of each large flower. Glue a 1/8" (2.5 mm) round pearl bead to the center of each flower.

7. Using the template below, make five leaves of Paper G. Position the flowers and leaves along the top of the bouquet paper, then glue.

8. Using the templates below, make two butterflies of Paper E. Glue four 1/16" (1.5 mm) round pear beads to each butterfly. Glue the butterflies to Paper B. Use the 1/8" (3 mm) circle craft punch to make four circles of Paper D. Glue a circle to each corner of Paper B to complete the card.

Full-Size Templates

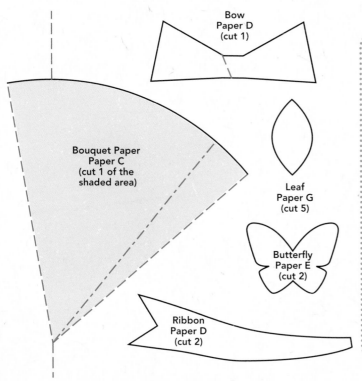

Bow
Paper D
(cut 1)

Bouquet Paper
Paper C
(cut 1 of the
shaded area)

Leaf
Paper G
(cut 5)

Butterfly
Paper E
(cut 2)

Ribbon
Paper D
(cut 2)

Close-Up View

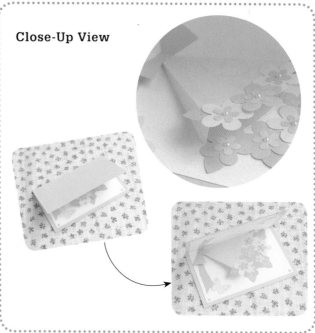

Vintage Greetings

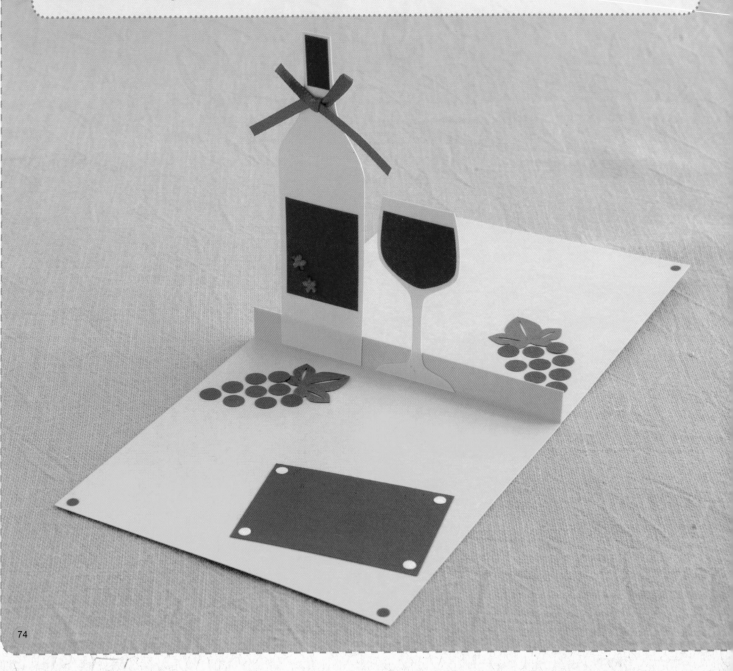

Materials

Paper A (pink):
Two 4" x 4 ¼" (10 x 11 cm) pieces
Paper B (light blue):
One 4 ¾" x 6 ¾" (12 x 17 cm) piece
Paper C (yellow):
One 4" x 4" (10 x 10 cm) piece
Paper D (orange):
One 2 ½" x 4" (6 x 10 cm) piece
Paper E (white):
One 1 ½" x 2" (2.5 x 5 cm) piece
Rhinestones: Two ¼" (5 mm) flower-shaped rhinestones in red
Ribbon: One ⅛" x 5 ½" (3 mm x 14 cm) piece in red

Tools

⅛" (3 mm) circle craft punch
¼" (6 mm) circle craft punch
Basic tools shown on page 10

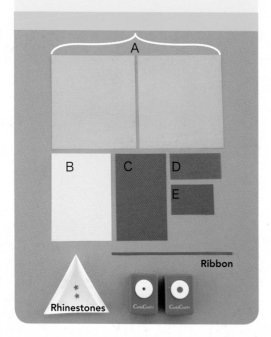

How It Works

The pop-up mechanism for this card is a center strip created by the two Paper A pieces.

Construction Diagram

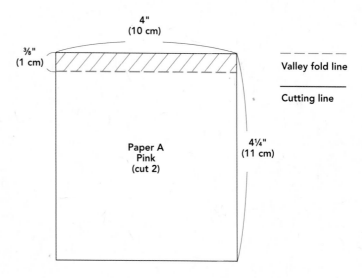

4"
(10 cm)

⅜"
(1 cm)

Paper A
Pink
(cut 2)

4¼"
(11 cm)

- - - - Valley fold line

——— Cutting line

*The construction diagram is shown at half-scale.

1. Fold the two Paper A pieces along the fold line, as shown in the construction diagram. Glue the two pieces together along the folded edges to create the pop-up mechanism.

2. Using the templates on page 77, make one bottle of Paper B and one cork and one label of Paper C. Glue the cork and label to the bottle. Tie the ribbon into a bow. Glue the bow to the bottle beneath the cork.

3. Using the templates on page 77, make one glass of Paper B and the wine of Paper C. Glue the wine to the glass.

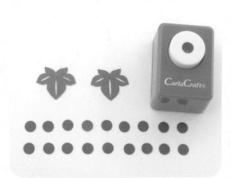

4. Using the template on page 77, make two leaves of Paper D. Use the ¼" (6 mm) circle craft punch to make eighteen circles of Paper C.

5. Make two grape clusters using nine circles and one leaf each. Glue the grape clusters to Paper B.

6. Glue the flower-shaped rhinestones to the label. Glue the bottle and glass to the pop-up mechanism of Paper A.

7. Glue Paper E to the lower right corner of Paper A. Use the ⅛" (3 mm) circle craft punch to make four circles of Paper B. Glue a circle to each corner of Paper E. Use the ⅛" (3 mm) circle craft punch to make four circles of Paper C. Glue a circle to each corner of Paper A to complete the card.

Full-Size Templates

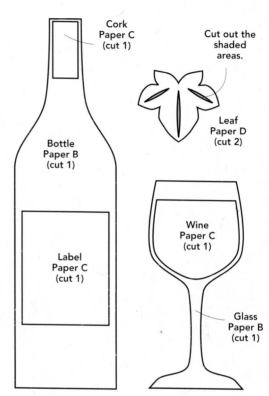

Cork
Paper C
(cut 1)

Cut out the shaded areas.

Leaf
Paper D
(cut 2)

Bottle
Paper B
(cut 1)

Wine
Paper C
(cut 1)

Label
Paper C
(cut 1)

Glass
Paper B
(cut 1)

Close-Up View

From a Little Bird

GREAT FOR • Valentine's Day • Party Invitation • Mother's Day • Get Well Soon • Thank You

Materials

Paper A (bright yellow):
One 3 ¾" x 4 ¾" (9.5 x 12 cm) piece
Paper B (bright green):
One 3 ¾" x 4 ¾" (9.5 x 12 cm) piece
Paper C (bright blue):
One 2 ¼" x 2 ½" (5.5 x 6.5 cm) piece
Paper D (blue):
One 2 ½" x 2 ½" (6 x 6 cm) piece
Paper E (yellow):
One 2" x 2" (5 x 5 cm) piece
Paper F (white):
One 2 ½" x 4" (6 x 10 cm) piece
Paper G (green):
One 2" x 2" (5 x 5 cm) piece
Rhinestone: One ⅛" (3 mm) heart-shaped
rhinestone in red

Tools

⅛" (3 mm) circle craft punch
³⁄₁₆" (5 mm) circle craft punch
Large daisy craft punch
Basic tools shown on page 10

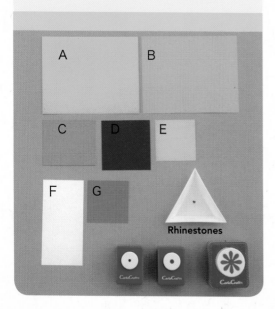

How It Works

The pop-up mechanism
for this card is a center
strip created by the
Paper A and B pieces.

Construction Diagram

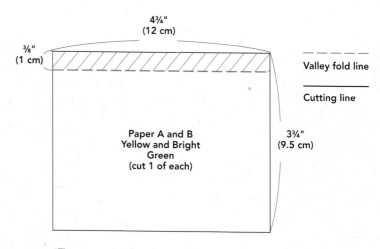

4¾"
(12 cm)

⅜"
(1 cm)

Valley fold line

Cutting line

Paper A and B
Yellow and Bright
Green
(cut 1 of each)

3¾"
(9.5 cm)

*The construction diagram is shown at half-scale.

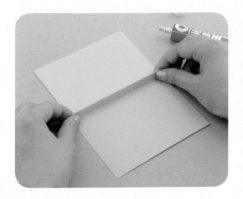

1. Fold the two Paper A pieces along the fold line, as shown in the construction diagram. Glue the two pieces together along the folded edges to create the pop-up mechanism.

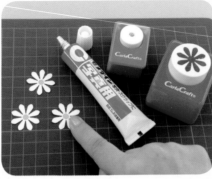

2. Use the large daisy craft punch to make three daisies of Paper F and the ³⁄₁₆" (5 mm) circle craft punch to make three circles of Paper E. Glue a circle to the center of each daisy.

3. Make two ¹⁄₁₆" x 1 ¼" (2 mm x 3 cm) and one ¹⁄₁₆" x 2" (2 mm x 5 cm) strips of Paper G to form stems. Using the template on page 81, make two flower pots of Paper D.

4. Glue a daisy to each stem, then glue the daisies to the wrong side of one flower pot. Glue the flower pot with the daisies to the pop-up mechanism of Paper B. Glue the other flower pot to the pop-up mechanism of Paper A to form the back side of the flower pot.

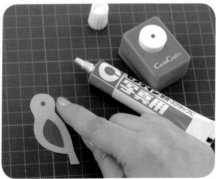

5. Using the templates on page 81, make one bird of Paper C and one wing of Paper D. Glue the wing to the bird. Use the ¹⁄₈" (3 mm) circle craft punch to make a circle of Paper D. Glue the circle to the bird to form the eye.

6. Using the templates on page 81, make one beak of Paper E and one envelope of Paper F. Glue the beak to the wrong side of the bird near the edge. Make a valley fold along the envelope fold line to form the flap, then glue the flap down. Glue the heart-shaped rhinestone to the envelope, then glue the envelope to the wrong side of the beak.

Full-Size Templates

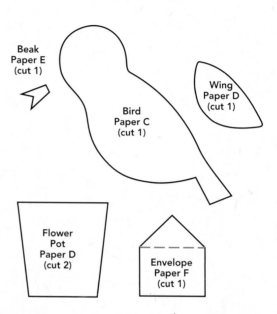

Beak
Paper E
(cut 1)

Bird
Paper C
(cut 1)

Wing
Paper D
(cut 1)

Flower
Pot
Paper D
(cut 2)

Envelope
Paper F
(cut 1)

7. Glue the finished bird to the pop-up mechanism of Paper B. Use the ⅛" (3 mm) circle craft punch to make seven circles of Paper G. Glue the circles to Paper B in a zigzag pattern to complete the card.

Close-Up View

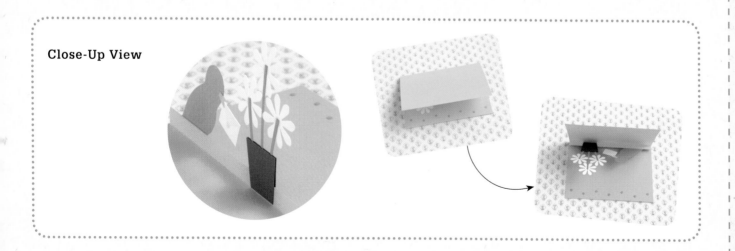

Sweet Salutations

GREAT FOR • Valentine's Day • Thank You

Materials

Paper A (brown):
One 5" x 7" (12.5 x 18 cm) piece
Paper B (brown):
One ¾" x 1 ½" (2 x 4 cm) piece
Paper C (white):
One 1 ¾" x 3 ¼" (4.5 x 8.5 cm) piece
Paper D (white):
One 2 ½" x 4" (6 x 10 cm) piece
Paper E (gold):
Two 1" x 1" (2.5 x 2.5 cm) pieces
Paper F (red):
Two ¾" x 1" (2 x 2.5 cm) pieces
Paper G (gold):
One ⅜" x ⅝" (1 x 1.5 cm) piece
Paper H (red):
 One 2 ¾" x 2 ¾" (7 x 7 cm) piece

Tools

Heart craft punch (with small and large hearts)
Pen: Gold gel pen
Basic tools shown on page 10

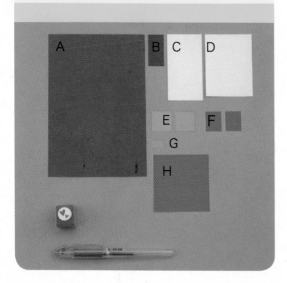

How It Works

The pop-up mechanism for this card is a convex triangle glued to the center of Paper A.

Close-Up View

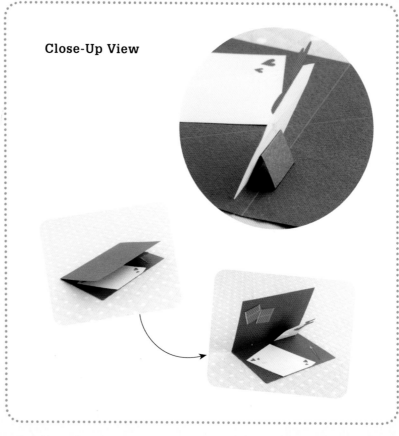

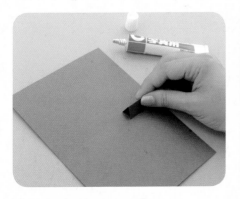
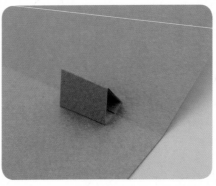

1. Fold Paper A in half lengthwise. Using the template on page 85, make the pop-up mechanism of Paper B. Glue the pop-up mechanism to Paper A along the center fold, about ¾" (2 cm) from the right edge.

2. Using the templates on page 85, make one envelope of Paper C and three hearts of Paper H.

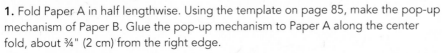

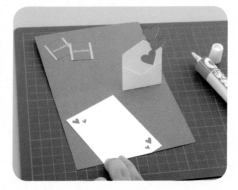

3. Make valley folds along the envelope fold lines to form the flap, then glue the envelope closed. Glue the hearts to the envelope, then glue the finished envelope to the pop-up mechanism of Paper B.

4. Glue each piece of Paper F to a piece of Paper E. Use the gold gel pen to write "chocolate" on each piece. Glue the finished chocolates to Paper A.

5. Using the template on page 85, make one letter of Paper D. Use the heart craft punch to make two small and two large hearts of Paper H. Glue the hearts to two corners of the letter. Position the slanted side of the letter along the front edge of Paper A and glue to secure.

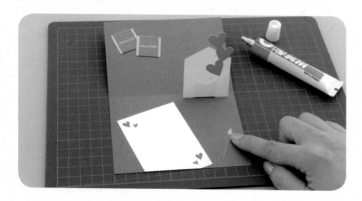

6. Using the templates below, make one pen of Paper H and one nib of Paper G. Glue the nib to the pen. Use a stylus to make a line on the nib. Glue the pen to Paper A to complete the card.

Full-Size Templates

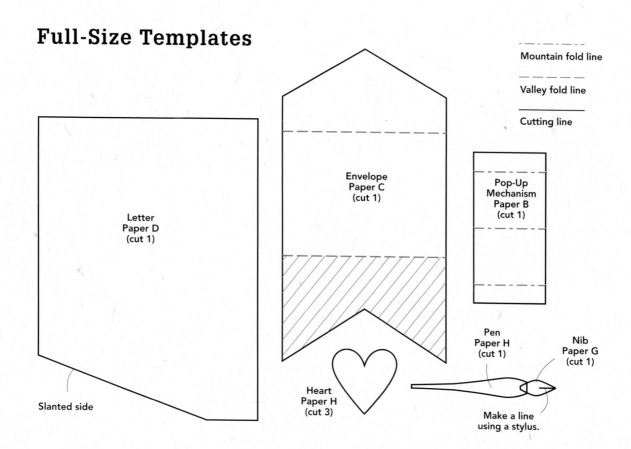

- - - - - - Mountain fold line

- - - - Valley fold line

———— Cutting line

Letter
Paper D
(cut 1)

Slanted side

Envelope
Paper C
(cut 1)

Pop-Up
Mechanism
Paper B
(cut 1)

Heart
Paper H
(cut 3)

Pen
Paper H
(cut 1)

Nib
Paper G
(cut 1)

Make a line
using a stylus.

Pansies & Ladybugs

GREAT FOR • Mother's Day • Get Well Soon • Thank You • Blank Greeting

Materials

Paper A (light green):
One 5" x 6 ¾" (12.5 x 17 cm) piece
Paper B (light purple):
One 1 ¾" x 3 ½" (4.5 x 9 cm) piece
Paper C (yellow):
One 2 ½" x 3 ¼" (6 x 8 cm) piece
Paper D (purple):
One 2 ½" x 3 ¼" (6 x 8 cm) piece
Paper E (green):
One 2 ½" x 2 ½" (6 x 6 cm) piece
Paper F (dark blue):
One 1 ¼" x 1 ¼" (3 x 3 cm) piece
Paper G (red):
One 1 ¼" x 1 ¼" (3 x 3 cm) piece
Paper H (white):
One 1 ½" x 2 ¼" (4 x 5.5 cm) piece
Rhinestones: Five ⅛" (3 mm) heart-shaped
rhinestones in yellow
Tape: Two 6 ¾" (17 cm) long pieces of
decorative tape in green

Tools

⅛" (3 mm) circle craft punch
³⁄₁₆" (5 mm) circle craft punch
Basic tools shown on page 10

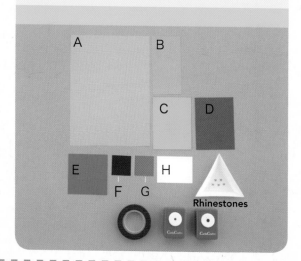

How It Works

The pop-up mecha-
nism for this card is
a convex flower pot
glued to the center of
Paper A.

Close-Up View

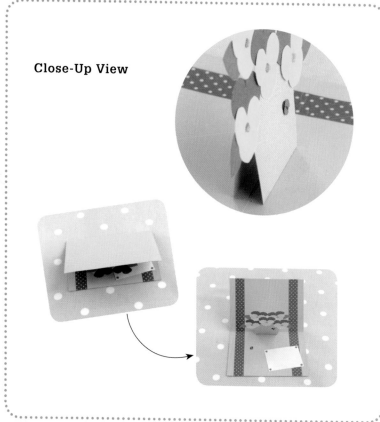

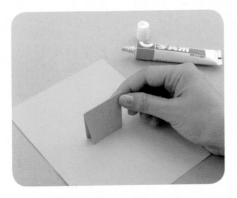

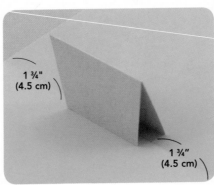

1. Fold Paper A in half lengthwise. Using the template on page 89, make the flower pot of Paper B. Glue the flower pot to Paper A along the center fold, about 1 ¾" (4.5 cm) from each edge.

2. Using the templates on page 89, make five Pansy A pieces of Paper D and five Pansy B pieces of Paper C. Make lines on the Pansy B pieces using a stylus. Overlap each Pansy A piece with a Pansy B piece and glue.

3. Position a heart-shaped rhinestone upside down and glue to the center of each pansy. Glue one pansy to the center of the flower pot, then glue the remaining pansies around this flower.

4. Make two ladybugs, as shown on page 89. Glue one ladybug to the flower pot and one to Paper A. Using the template on page 89, make four leaves of Paper E. Make lines on each leaf using a stylus. Glue the leaves to the wrong side of the pansies.

5. Adhere each piece of tape to Paper A, about ⅜" (1 cm) from each edge. Trim any excess tape.

6. Glue Paper H to the lower right corner of Paper A at a slight angle (Paper H will overlap the tape on one side). Use the ⅛" (3 mm) circle craft punch to make four circles of Paper E. Glue a circle to each corner of Paper H to complete the card.

Full-Size Templates

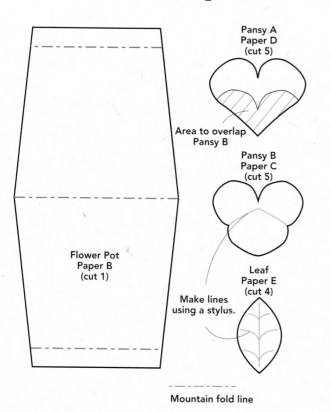

Pansy A
Paper D
(cut 5)

Area to overlap
Pansy B

Pansy B
Paper C
(cut 5)

Flower Pot
Paper B
(cut 1)

Make lines
using a stylus.

Leaf
Paper E
(cut 4)

- - - - - - - Mountain fold line

———— Cutting line

How to Make a Lady Bug

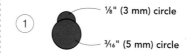

(1)   ⅛" (3 mm) circle
    ³⁄₁₆" (5 mm) circle

Use the ⅛" (3 mm) circle craft punch to make a circle of Paper F and the ³⁄₁₆" (5 mm) circle craft punch to make a circle of Paper F. Overlap the circles and glue together to form the body.

(2)   ³⁄₁₆" (5 mm) circle

Use the ³⁄₁₆" (5 mm) circle craft punch to make a circle of Paper G. Cut the circle in half to form two semi-circles.

(3)   Glue the two Paper G semi-circles to the Paper F pieces to form wings.

Mountain View Message

GREAT FOR • Bon Voyage • Thank You • Blank Greeting

Materials

Paper A (bright blue):
One 5" x 7" (12.5 x 18 cm) piece
Paper B (blue):
One 2 ¾" x 5 ½" (7 x 14 cm) piece
Paper C (red):
One 1 ½" (4 cm) in diameter circular piece
Paper D (white):
One ¾" x 1 ½" (2 x 4 cm) piece
Paper E (bright green):
One ⅝" x 2" (1.5 x 5 cm) piece
Paper F (green):
One 2" x 4" (5 x 10 cm) piece

Tools

Basic tools shown on page 10

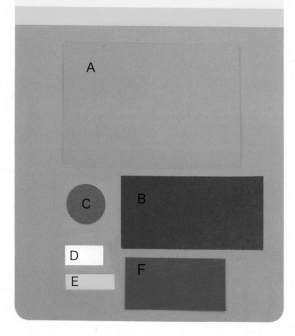

How It Works

The pop-up mechanism for this card is a convex volcano glued to Paper A.

Close-Up View

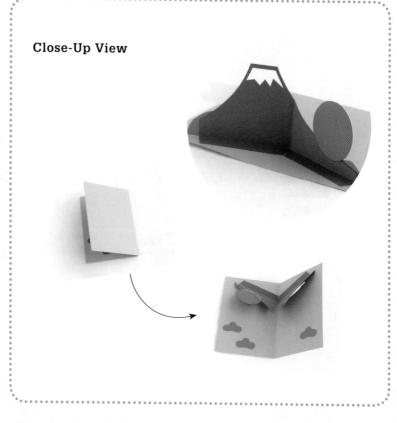

 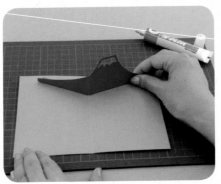

1. Fold Paper A in half widthwise. Using the template on page 93, make one volcano of Paper B. Make mountain folds along the volcano fold lines.

2. Glue the volcano to Paper A, about 1 ½" (3.5 cm) from the back edge of Paper A with the volcano folds forming 70° angles with the center fold.

 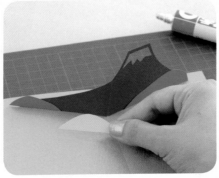 

3. Using the templates on page 93, make one cloud of Paper D, one Mountain A of Paper E, one Mountain B, one Mountain C, and three trees of Paper F.

4. Glue Mountains B and C to the volcano, then overlap Mountain A with Mountain C and glue.

5. Glue the three trees of Paper F to Paper A.

6. Glue the cloud to the right side of the volcano and Paper C to the wrong side of the volcano to complete the card.

Full-Size Templates

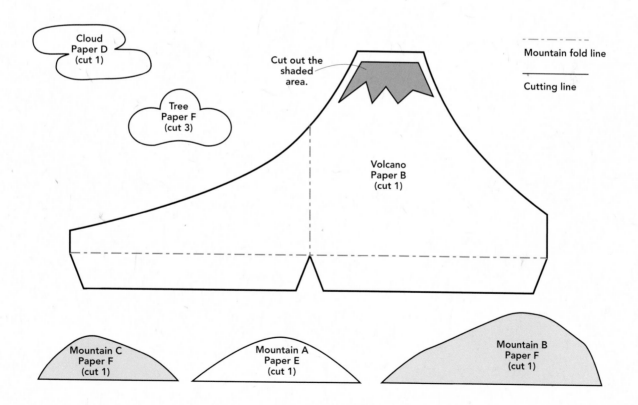

Cloud
Paper D
(cut 1)

Tree
Paper F
(cut 3)

Cut out the
shaded
area.

Mountain fold line

Cutting line

Volcano
Paper B
(cut 1)

Mountain C
Paper F
(cut 1)

Mountain A
Paper E
(cut 1)

Mountain B
Paper F
(cut 1)

Father's Day Classic

Materials

Paper A (cream):
One 5" x 6 ¾" (12.5 x 17 cm) piece

Paper B (light brown):
One 6" x 6" (15 x 15 cm) piece

Paper C (dark brown):
One 2 ¾" x 2 ¾" (7 x 7 cm) piece

Paper D (cream):
One 1 ½" x 2 ¾" (3.5 x 7 cm) piece

Tools

⅛" (3 mm) circle craft punch
³⁄₁₆" (5 mm) circle craft punch
Basic tools shown on page 10

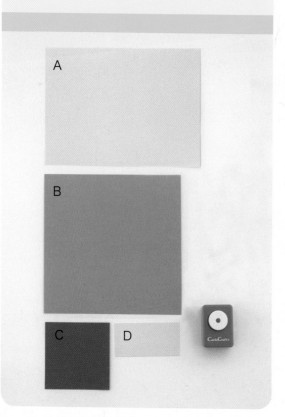

How It Works

The pop-up mechanism for this card is a convex V-shaped piece glued to the center of Paper A.

Close-Up View

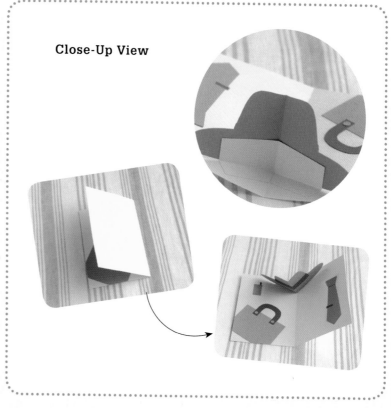

 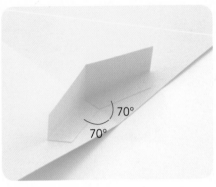 

1. Fold Paper A in half widthwise. Using the template on page 97, make one pop-up mechanism of Paper D. Make mountain folds along the pop-up mechanism fold lines. Glue the pop-up mechanism to Paper A, about 1" (2.5 cm) from the back edge of Paper A with the pop-up mechanism folds forming 70° angles with the center fold.

2. Using the templates on page 97, make one hat of Paper B and one ribbon of Paper C. Glue the ribbon to the hat.

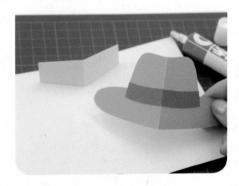  

3. Glue the finished hat to the pop-up mechanism.

4. Using the templates on page 97, make one briefcase of Paper B and one handle of Paper C. Glue the briefcase to Paper A, then glue the handle to the briefcase. Use the ³⁄₁₆" (5 mm) circle craft punch to make two circles of Paper B. Glue the circles to the handle.

5. Using the templates on page 97, make one cell phone of Paper B and one antenna of Paper C. Glue the antenna to the wrong side of the cell phone. Glue the finished cell phone to Paper A.

6. Using the templates below, make one tie top of Paper B, one tie bottom of Paper B, and one tie clip of Paper C. Glue the tie bottom to Paper B, then glue the tie top to the tie bottom. Glue the tie clip to the bottom to complete the card.

Full-Size Templates

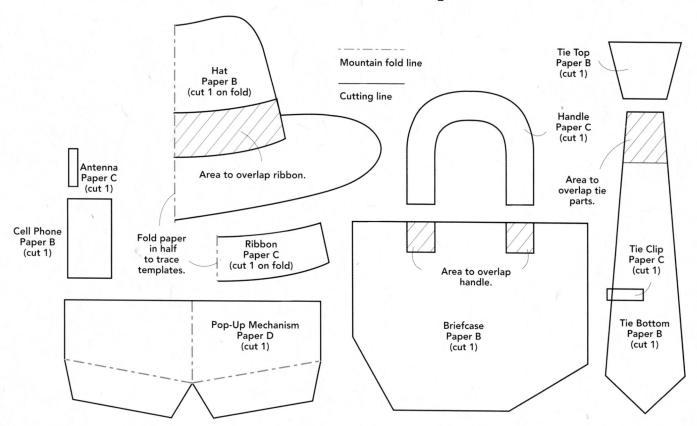

Hat
Paper B
(cut 1 on fold)

Area to overlap ribbon.

Mountain fold line

Cutting line

Tie Top
Paper B
(cut 1)

Handle
Paper C
(cut 1)

Area to overlap tie parts.

Antenna
Paper C
(cut 1)

Cell Phone
Paper B
(cut 1)

Fold paper in half to trace templates.

Ribbon
Paper C
(cut 1 on fold)

Area to overlap handle.

Tie Clip
Paper C
(cut 1)

Pop-Up Mechanism
Paper D
(cut 1)

Briefcase
Paper B
(cut 1)

Tie Bottom
Paper B
(cut 1)

Piece of Cake

GREAT FOR • Birthday • Party Invitation

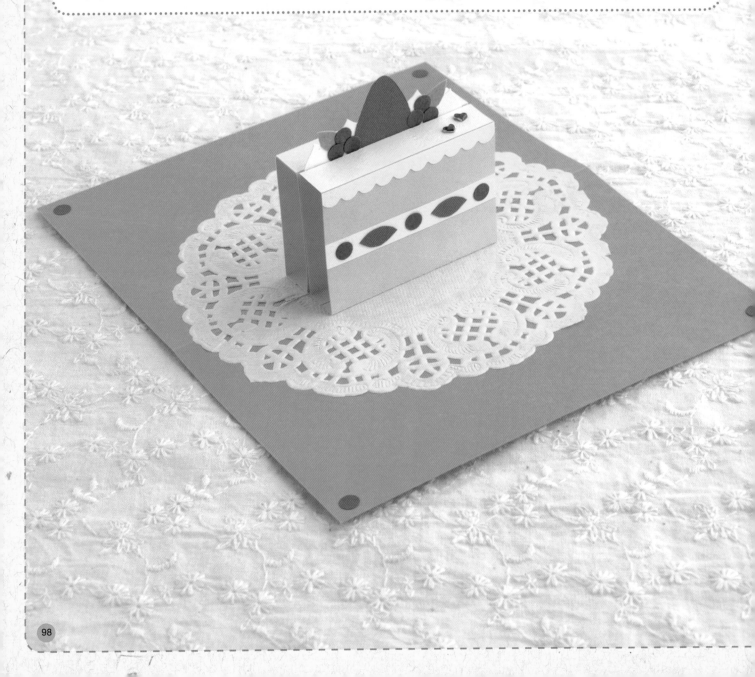

Materials

Paper A (pink):
One 5" x 6 ¼" (12.5 x 16 cm) piece
Paper B (cream):
Two 2" x 3 ½" (5 x 9 cm) pieces
Paper C (white):
One 2" x 2 ¾" (5 x 7 cm) piece
Paper D (red):
One 2" x 2" (5 x 5 cm) piece
Paper E (blue):
One 2" x 2" (5 x 5 cm) piece
Paper F (green):
One 1 ¼" x 1 ¼" (3 x 3 cm) piece
Doily:
One 4 ½" (11.5 cm) in diameter white doily
Rhinestones: Two ⅛" (3 mm) heart-shaped
rhinestones in red

Tools

³⁄₁₆" (5 mm) circle craft punch
Basic tools shown on page 10

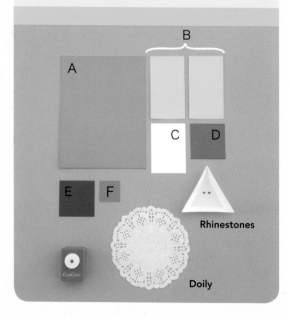

How It Works

The pop-up mechanism for this card is a convex piece of cake glued to the center of Paper A.

Close-Up View

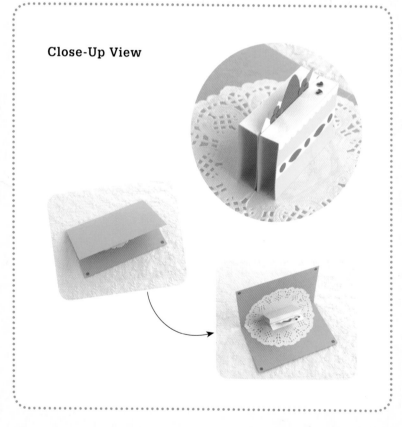

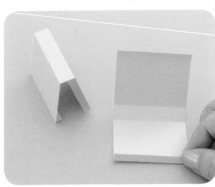

1. Fold Paper A in half lengthwise. Fold the doily in half and glue to Paper A, aligning both papers at the center fold.

2. Using the template on page 101, make two cake pieces of Paper B. Make mountain folds along the cake fold lines.

3. Glue the cake pieces to the center of the doily, about 1 ½" (3.7 cm) from each edge of Paper A.

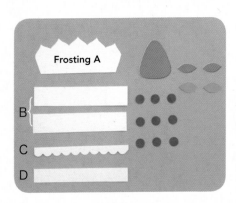

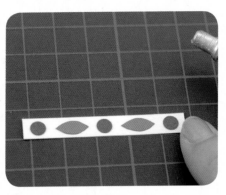

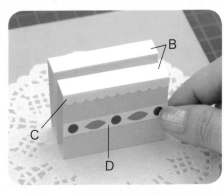

4. Using the templates on page 101, make one Frosting A piece, two Frosting B pieces, one Frosting C piece, and one Frosting D piece of Paper C, one Strawberry A and two Strawberry B pieces of Paper D, and two leaves of Paper F. Use the ³⁄₁₆" (5 mm) circle craft punch to make nine circles of Paper E.

5. Glue three circles and the two Strawberry B pieces to Frosting D.

6. Glue the finished Frosting D piece, the Frosting C piece, and the two Frosting B pieces to the cake pieces.

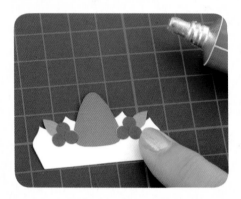 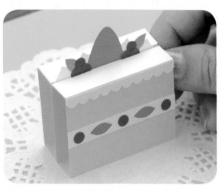 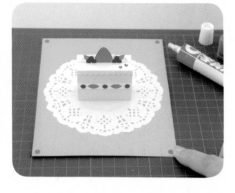

7. Glue Strawberry A to Frosting A. Glue three circles and one leaf to Frosting A on each side of the strawberry.

8. Insert the finished Frosting A piece between the two cake pieces and glue.

9. Glue the two heart-shaped rhinestones to the top of the finished cake. Use the ³⁄₁₆" (5 mm) circle craft punch to make four circles of Paper D. Glue a circle to each corner of Paper A to complete the card.

Full-Size Templates

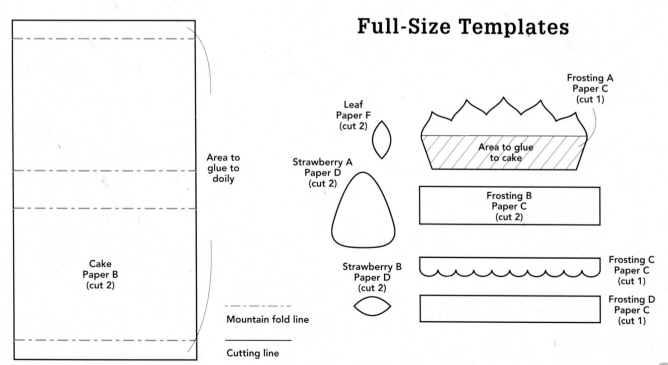

Cake
Paper B
(cut 2)

Area to glue to doily

Mountain fold line

Cutting line

Leaf
Paper F
(cut 2)

Strawberry A
Paper D
(cut 2)

Strawberry B
Paper D
(cut 2)

Frosting A
Paper C
(cut 1)

Area to glue to cake

Frosting B
Paper C
(cut 2)

Frosting C
Paper C
(cut 1)

Frosting D
Paper C
(cut 1)

Holiday Lights

GREAT FOR • Holiday/Christmas • Party Invitation

Materials

Paper A (dark blue):
One 5 ¼" x 6 ¼" (13 x 17 cm) piece
Paper B (bright blue):
One 4 ¾" x 6 ¼" (12 x 16 cm) piece
Paper C (yellow):
One 2" x 2" (5 x 5 cm) piece
Paper D (green):
One 1 ½" x 2" (4 x 5 cm) piece
Beads:
Six ¹⁄₁₆" (2 mm) round pearl beads in white

Tools

Pen: White gel pen
Basic tools shown on page 10

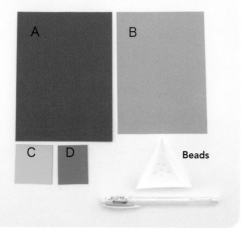

How It Works

The pop-up mechanisms for this card are convex buildings located on Paper B.

Close-Up View

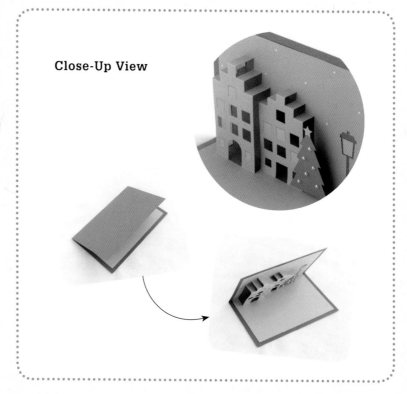

 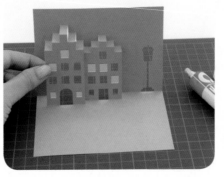 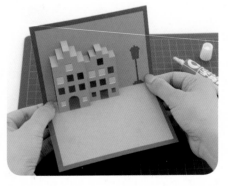

1. Fold Paper A in half lengthwise. Using the template on page 105, make one inner piece of Paper B.

2. Fold the inner piece along the fold lines. Make seven ⅜" (1 cm) squares of Paper C and glue them to the wrong side of the windows.

3. Align Papers A and B at the center fold and glue together, making sure to keep the pop-up mechanism of Paper B unattached.

4. Using the templates on page 105, make one star and one streetlight of Paper C and one tree of Paper D. Glue the round pearl beads to the tree.

5. Glue the streetlight to Paper A at the corresponding cut out area. Glue the finished tree to the building on the right. Use the white gel pen to draw snowflakes on the background of Paper B to complete the card.

Full-Size Templates

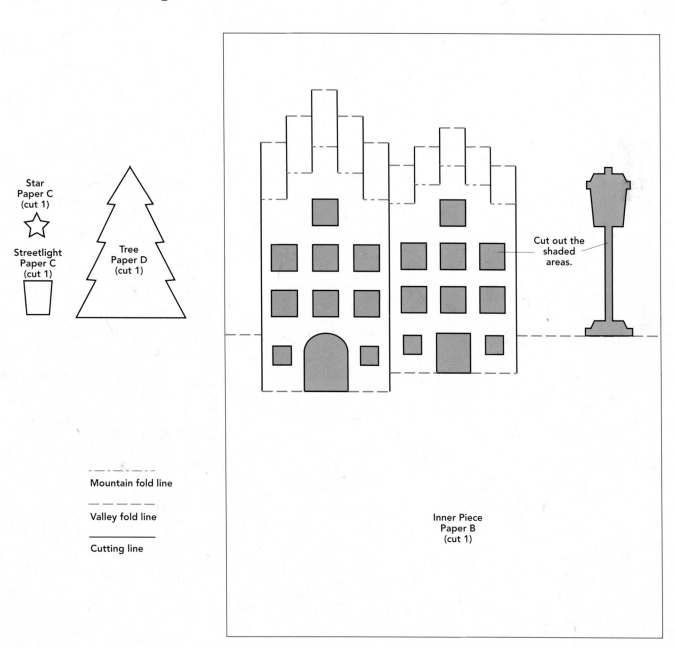

Star
Paper C
(cut 1)

Streetlight
Paper C
(cut 1)

Tree
Paper D
(cut 1)

Cut out the
shaded
areas.

Inner Piece
Paper B
(cut 1)

Mountain fold line

Valley fold line

Cutting line

A Heartfelt Note

GREAT FOR • Wedding Invitation • Valentine's Day • Mother's Day

Materials

Paper A (white):
one 4 ¾" x 7" (12 x 18 cm) piece
Paper B (pink):
One 4" x 6 ¼" (10 x 16 cm) piece
Paper C (white):
One 1 ½" x 4 ¾" (4 x 12 cm) piece
Paper D (pink):
One 1 ¼" x 1 ¼" (3 x 3 cm) piece

Tools

⅛" (3 mm) circle craft punch
Basic tools shown on page 10

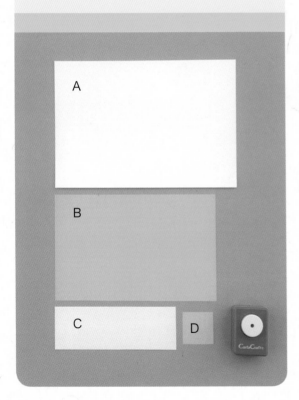

How It Works

The pop-up mechanism for this card is a convex heart located on Paper B.

Close-Up View

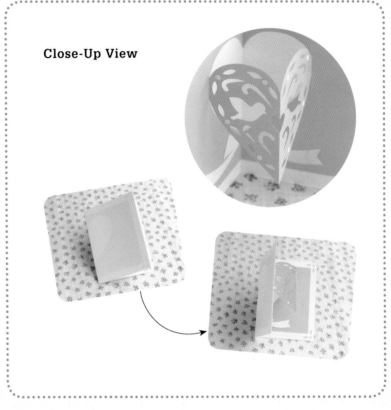

1. Fold Papers A and B in half widthwise.

2. Using the template on page 109, make one inner piece of Paper B, keeping Paper B folded in half. Make sure to reserve the leaf-shaped motifs cut out of Paper B.

3. Fold the inner piece along the fold lines. Align Papers A and B at the center fold and glue together, making sure to keep the pop-up mechanism of Paper B unattached.

4. Using the templates on page 109, make one Ribbon A and two Ribbon B pieces of Paper C. Glue the Ribbon B pieces to Paper B on each side of the center fold. Glue Ribbon A on top of the Ribbon B pieces.

5. Use the ⅛" (3 mm) circle craft punch to make eight circles of Paper C. Glue the circles around the heart on the inner piece.

6. Use the ⅛" (3 mm) circle craft punch to make four circles of Paper D. Glue a circle and two of the reserved leaf-shaped motifs to each corner of Paper A to complete the card.

Full-Size Templates

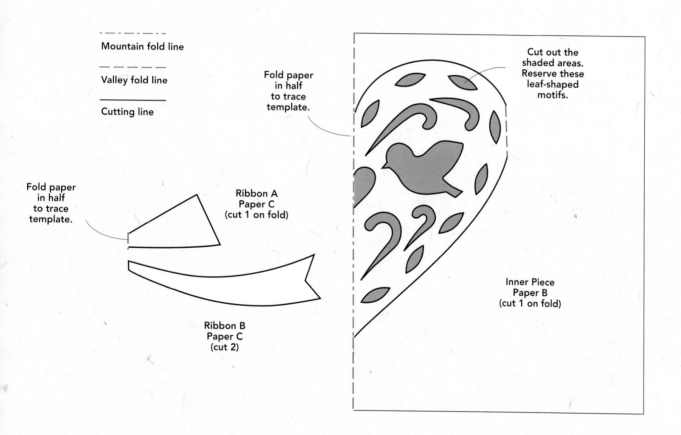

Mountain fold line

Valley fold line

Cutting line

Fold paper
in half
to trace
template.

Cut out the
shaded areas.
Reserve these
leaf-shaped
motifs.

Fold paper
in half
to trace
template.

Ribbon A
Paper C
(cut 1 on fold)

Ribbon B
Paper C
(cut 2)

Inner Piece
Paper B
(cut 1 on fold)

Letters of Gratitude

GREAT FOR • Thank You

Materials

Paper A (blue):
One 5 ¼" x 6" (13.5 x 15 cm) piece
Paper B (bright green):
One 5" x 5 ½" (12.5 x 14 cm) piece
Paper C (white):
One 2" x 2" (5 x 5 cm) piece
Paper D (yellow):
One 2" x 2" (5 x 5 cm) piece

Tools

Small butterfly craft punch
⅛" (3 mm) circle craft punch
Small flower craft punch
Basic tools shown on page 10

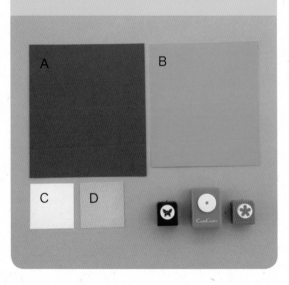

How It Works

The pop-up mechanism for this card is the phrase "Thank You" located on Paper B.

Close-Up View

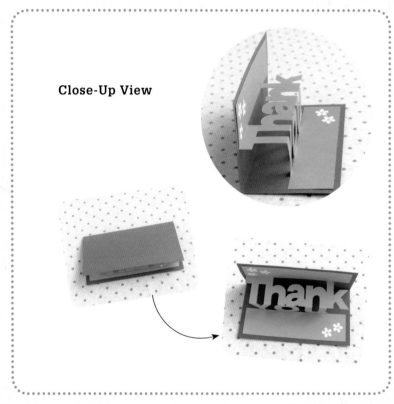

  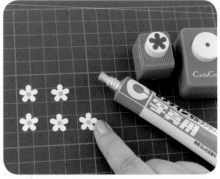

1. Fold Paper A in half lengthwise. Using the template on page 113, make one inner piece of Paper B.

2. Fold the inner piece along the fold lines. Align Papers A and B at the center fold and glue together, making sure to keep the pop-up mechanism of Paper B unattached.

3. Use the small flower craft punch to make five flowers of Paper C and the 1/8" (3 mm) craft punch to make five circles of Paper D. Glue a circle to the center of each flower.

4. Glue the finished flowers to Paper B.

5. Use the small butterfly craft punch to make two butterflies of Paper D. Glue one butterfly to the inner piece and one to Paper A to complete the card.

Full-Size Template

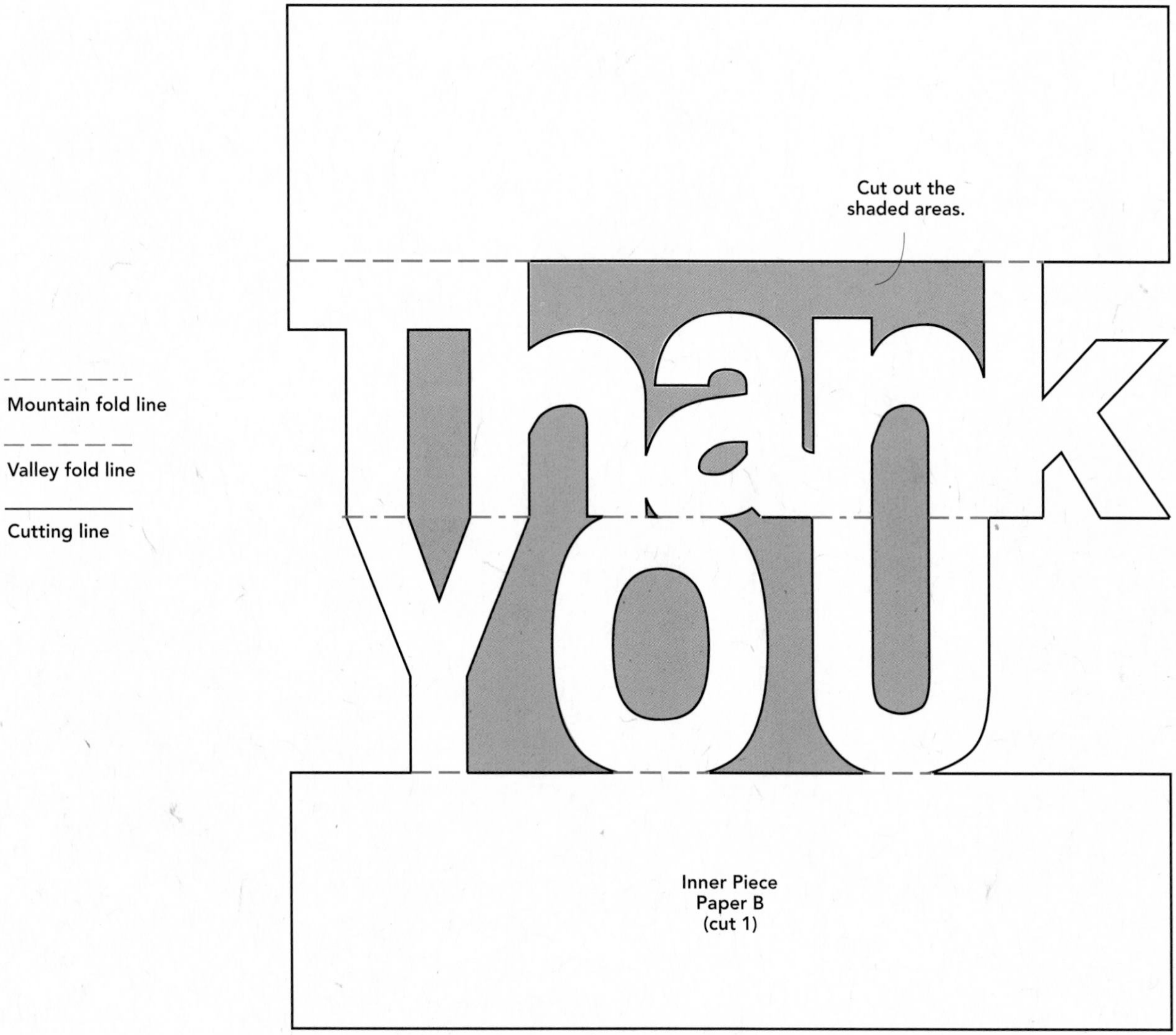

Cut out the
shaded areas.

thank
you

Mountain fold line

Valley fold line

Cutting line

Inner Piece
Paper B
(cut 1)

Lucky Charms

GREAT FOR • Good Luck • Bon Voyage • St. Patrick's Day • Thank You

Materials

Paper A (light yellow):
One 5 ½" x 5 ½" (14 x 14 cm) piece
Paper B (green):
One 4" x 4" (10 x 10 cm) piece
Paper C (green):
One 2" x 4" (5 x 10 cm) piece
Paper D (black):
One ¾" x 1 ½" (2 x 4 cm) piece
Paper E (red):
One ¾" x 1 ½" (2 x 4 cm) piece
Paper F (yellow):
One 1 ½" x 3 ¼" (4 x 8 cm) piece
Rhinestones:
Twelve ⅟₁₆" (1.5 mm) round black rhinestones
in black

Tools

⅛" (3 mm) circle craft punch
Basic tools shown on page 10

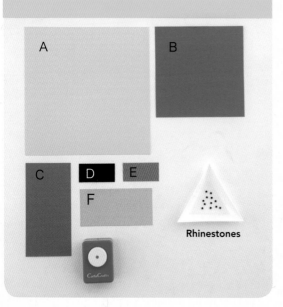

Close-Up View

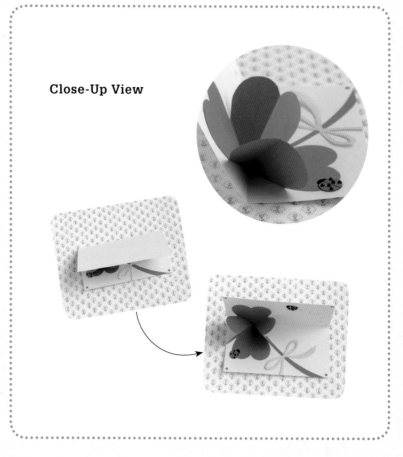

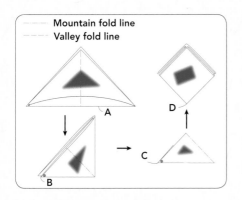

1. Fold Paper B into fourths, as shown in the above diagram. **A.** Fold Paper B in half. Fold in half again using a valley fold. **B.** Fold in half a third time using a mountain fold. **C.** The mountain fold will be on the right side of the triangle. **D.** Unfold Paper B completely and fold in half lengthwise, then widthwise to create a square.

2. Using the template on page 117, make one four leaf clover of the folded Paper B.

3. Fold Paper A in half lengthwise, Using the templates on page 117, make one stem of Paper C and one bow of Paper F. Glue the stem to Paper A, about ¼" (5 mm) from the right edge.

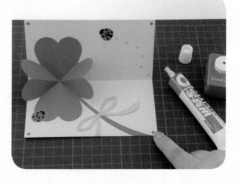

4. Glue the four leaf clover to the top of the stem. Close Paper A slightly and glue the top leaf to the background of Paper A.

5. Using the templates on page 117, make two Ladybug A pieces of Paper D and two Ladybug B pieces of Paper E. Glue the Ladybug B pieces to the Ladybug A pieces, as shown in the above photo. Glue six round black rhinestones to each ladybug.

6. Glue one ladybug to the background of Paper A and one to the four leaf clover. Use the ⅛" (3 mm) circle craft punch to make six circles of Paper F and four circles of Paper C. Glue the six circles of Paper F to the background of Paper A. Glue a circle of Paper C to each corner of Paper A to complete the card.

Full-Size Templates

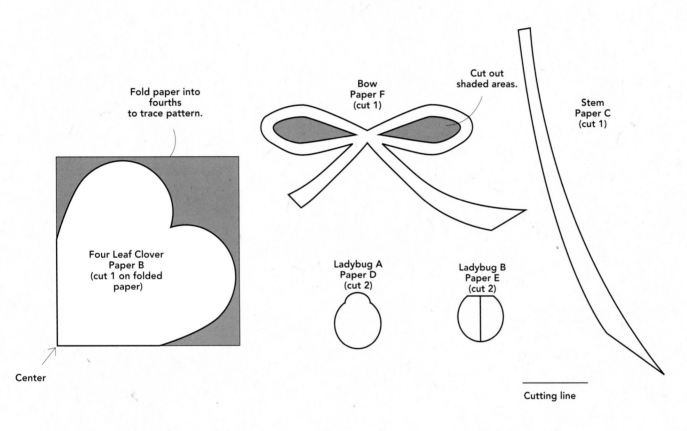

Fold paper into
fourths
to trace pattern.

Four Leaf Clover
Paper B
(cut 1 on folded
paper)

Center

Bow
Paper F
(cut 1)

Cut out
shaded areas.

Ladybug A
Paper D
(cut 2)

Ladybug B
Paper E
(cut 2)

Stem
Paper C
(cut 1)

Cutting line

Wish Upon A Star

GREAT FOR • Birthday • Party Invitation • Good Luck • Thank You

Materials

Paper A (light yellow):
One 5 ¼" x 7" (13 x 18 cm) piece
Paper B (gold):
One 4" x 4" (10 x 10 cm) piece
Paper C (pink):
One 1 ½" x 2 ¼" (4 x 5.5 cm) piece
Paper D (yellow):
One 1 ¼" x 1 ¼" (3 x 3 cm) piece
Wire:
One 1 ½" (3.5 cm) piece of 26-gauge wire
Ribbon:
One 4" (10 cm) piece of raffia ribbon in white
Beads:
Five ¹⁄₁₆" (2 mm) round pearl beads in pink
One ⅛" (3 mm) heart-shaped bead in pink

Tools

Star craft punch (with small and large stars)
⅛" (3 mm) circle craft punch
Basic tools shown on page 10

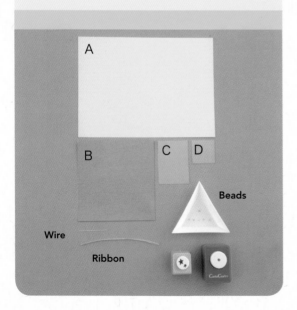

Close-Up View

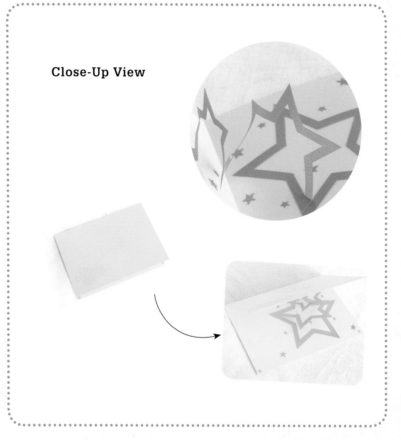

1. Fold Paper A in half widthwise. Using the template on page 121, make one star of Paper B.

2. Using the template on page 121, make one girl of Paper C. Tie the ribbon into a bow and glue the bow to the girl's waist. Glue the round pearl beads and the heart-shaped bead to the girl.

3. Glue the girl to Paper A. Glue the piece of wire to the girl's hand. Glue the center of the star to the other end of the wire.

4. Glue the outer layer of the star to Paper A.

5. Use the star craft punch to make seven small and seven large stars of Paper G. Glue the stars to Paper A.

6. Use the ⅛" (3 mm) circle craft punch to make four circles of Paper D. Glue a circle to each corner of Paper A to complete the card.

Full-Size Templates

Girl
Paper C
(cut 1)

Cut out the
shaded areas.

Star
Paper B
(cut 1)

Center of the star

Outer layer of
the star

Cutting line

Adding Messages to Your Cards

Create playful cards with a personal touch by mixing and matching card designs and messages. Most of the pop-up card designs in this book are suitable for multiple occasions, so a variety of messages and greetings can be applied to each design.

In some cases you may choose to handwrite your greeting, or instead you might want to use a typed message with a favorite computer font. Printing a typed message is great solution for making multiples of a card. Also, a typed message allows you to change the size of the font, which is helpful for fitting messages on small pieces of paper.

Customize Your Card

The "Teacup Bouquet" card on page 18 is an example of a versatile design suitable for many occasions. Deliver your message on paper of assorted shapes and sizes:

"Happy Birthday" is framed in a rectangle and accented by a border.

"Thank You" is featured on a miniature banner with curved lettering.

"Get Well" is printed on a rectangle with room for a handwritten note.

Here are some examples for adding messages and greetings to the card designs in this book:

"Happy Birthday"
Project on page 22

"Thank You"
Project on page 30

"Happy Halloween"
Project on page 50

"Happy Easter"
Project on page 54

"Bon Voyage"
Project on page 58

"Happy Valentine's Day"
Project on page 82

"Wishing You A Merry Christmas"
Project on page 102

"Congratulations on Your Wedding"
Project on page 106

"Good Luck"
Project on page 114

Decorating Your Cards

All the pop-up excitement may take place inside the card, but don't forget about decorating the front of the card. After all, this is the first thing someone will see when they open the envelope. Start with the pop-up templates, then embellish with ribbon, rhinestones, and decorative tape for a design that coordinates with the inside of the card. Use these designs or be inspired to create your own!

Embellishing Your Cards

The possibilities are endless when it comes to embellishing your cards. These designs incorporate ribbon for added texture and dimension.

"Bouquet of Balloons"
Project on page 30

"Letters of Gratitude"
Project on page 110

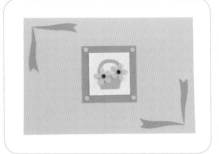

"Spring Salutations"
Project on page 54

"Sea View for You"
Project on page 58

"Fan with Cherry Blossoms"
Project on page 66

"From a Little Bird"
Project on page 78

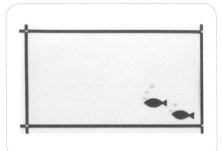

"Sweet Salutations"
Project on page 82

"Pansies & Ladybugs"
Project on page 86

"A Heartfelt Note"
Project on page 106

"Lucky Charms"
Project on page 114

"Teacup Bouquet"
Project on page 18

Getting Creative with the Templates

In addition to making all the wonderful pop-up card designs included in this book, you can use the full-size templates to craft a wide variety of paper goods. Here are some creative ideas to get you started, but remember, the possibilities are endless!

Idea 1   Menus, Message Boards, and Scrapbook Pages

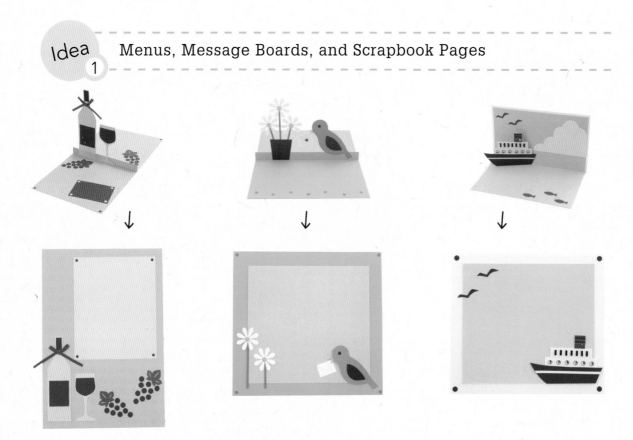

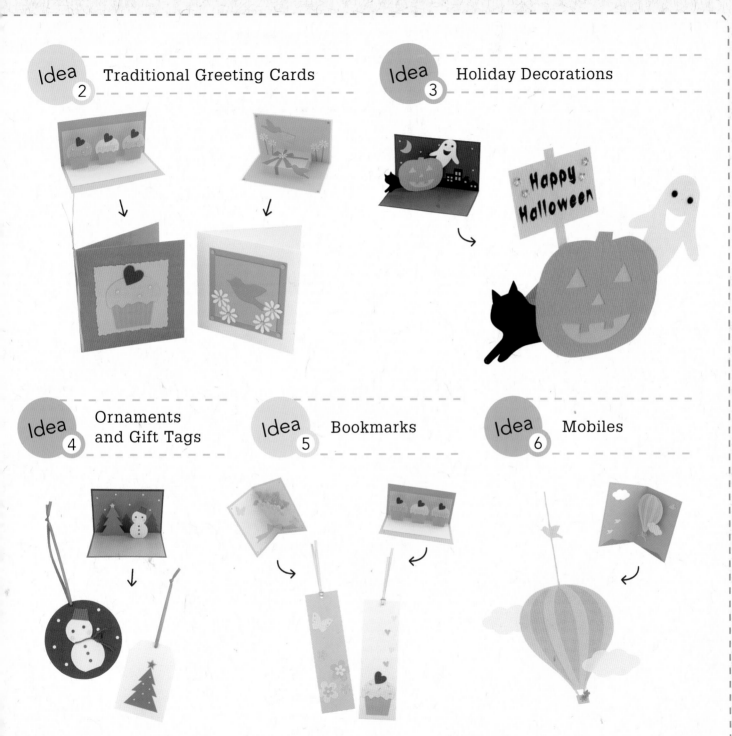

Idea 2 — Traditional Greeting Cards

Idea 3 — Holiday Decorations

Idea 4 — Ornaments and Gift Tags

Idea 5 — Bookmarks

Idea 6 — Mobiles

Happy Halloween

Craft Punch Reference

Carla Craft® craft punches are used throughout this book. However, you can use any brand that makes similarly sized and shaped craft punches as listed in the tools section for each project. When shopping for craft punches, use this actual-size reference as a guide.

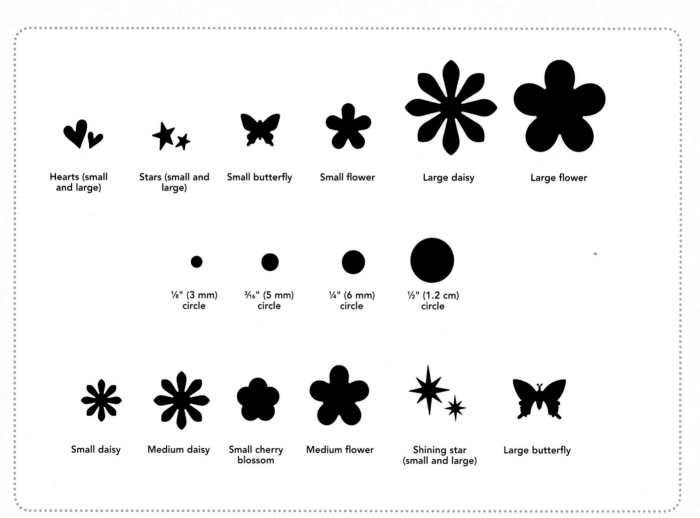

Hearts (small and large)   **Stars (small and large)**   **Small butterfly**   **Small flower**   **Large daisy**   **Large flower**

⅛" (3 mm) circle   ³⁄₁₆" (5 mm) circle   ¼" (6 mm) circle   ½" (1.2 cm) circle

Small daisy   **Medium daisy**   **Small cherry blossom**   **Medium flower**   **Shining star (small and large)**   **Large butterfly**